A Colourful Journey
Patchwork and Quilting
Book Number 5

Kaffe Fassett • Roberta Horton • Mary Mashuta
Liza Prior Lucy • Pauline Smith • Sally B Davis
Susan Druding • Brandon Mably • Sandy Donabed

A   R O W A N   P U B L I C A T I O N

First Published in Great Britain in 2003 by
Rowan Yarns
Green Lane Mill
Holmfirth
West Yorkshire
England
HD9 2DX

Art Director:	Kaffe Fassett
Technical editors:	Ruth Eglington and Pauline Smith
Co-ordinator:	Pauline Smith
Editorial Director:	Kate Buller
Patchwork Designs:	Kaffe Fassett, Liza Prior Lucy, Pauline Smith, Roberta Horton, Mary Mashuta, Sally B Davis, Brandon Mably, Sandy Donabed and Susan Druding.
Quilters:	Judy Irish and Terry Clark
Photographer:	Debbie Patterson
Styling:	Kaffe Fassett
Design Layout:	Fizz Design
Illustrations:	Ruth Eglinton
Feature:	Susan Druding
Cover Photography:	Joey Toller
Cover Styling:	Kim Hargreaves
Silk Flowers & Plants:	Bloom Tel: 0870 2414087

British Library Cataloguing in Publication Data
Rowan Yarns
Patchwork and Quilting
ISBN 1-904485-07-3

Colour reproduction by Chroma Graphics (Overseas) Pte. Ltd
Printed and bound in Singapore by KHL Printing Co. Pte. Ltd

CONTENTS

INTRODUCTION

Welcome to 'A Colourful Journey'.

My biggest pleasure in styling this latest Rowan Patchwork book was being able to use my family seaside house in Hastings as a backdrop for photographing this new and exciting collection of patchwork quilts.

The English seaside town of Hastings has long attracted artists but in the past few years is experiencing a new popularity. It possesses many charming parks and flamboyantly multi coloured houses draped across dramatic hillsides facing the English channel.

We have been working on the house for a year and it ís with great pride that I see the grand old lady, built in 1860, make her first appearance as a location. The soft pastel tones I used throughout this house were in response to the pearly quality of the reflected sea light.

A large primitive mural dominated two walls of the expansive drawing room, one of which was painted over, the other I completely reworked. The curtains in the drawing room are huge patchworks of small prints on cream checkerboard with pastel florals, some of which are old handkerchiefs. To lighten the rather dark kitchen I made over four hundred blue and white tiles at the Highland Stoneware Pottery in Scotland to completely re-tile this room.

I hope you find all the settings I have chosen do justice to the quilts contained in this book. I for my part certainly found it intensely stimulating and rewarding to see all these quiltmakers using my collection of fabrics in such diverse ways. Several of us in the design team seem to have been drawn to baby quilts; if you like them but want them bigger do expand the ideas. On the other hand many could be miniaturized to make handsome cushions.

The highlight for me in this publication is the chance to see and read about my favourite black quilt maker, Anna Williams. Susan Druding, known across America for her brilliant yarn store, Straw Into Gold in Oakland California, spent time with Anna and gives us the history of this remarkable talent who freed up and influenced so many designers.

Thanks to Debbie Patterson who photographed the projects so lovingly and to Lone Ormonde, a neighbour, who offered the use of her richly decorated house where we photographed two of the quilts. Last but not least a big thank you to a great team who made this book possible.

Kaffe Fassett

Chintz Flowerbeds
by Kaffe Fassett

Beyond The Pale
by Brandon Mably

This page Handkerchief Corner Pastel by Kaffe Fassett opposite, Fizz by Pauline Smith.

Extended Pinwheels
by Kaffe Fassett

Co-ordinated Chaos
by Sally B Davis

Fiesta quilt
by Kaffe Fassett

This page Tuscan table runner & Placemats by Liza Prior Lucy,
opposite Pete's Paul Quilt by Roberta Horton

Barcelona Tiles
by Mary Mashuta

21

Strippy Chevrons
by Susan Druding

Handkerchief Corner Dark
by Kaffe Fassett

24

SPRING COTTA

*This page
Baby
Lozenge
Quilt,
opposite,
Mosaic
Columns
both by
Kaffe
Fassett*

26

*Musetta by
Liza Prior Lucy*

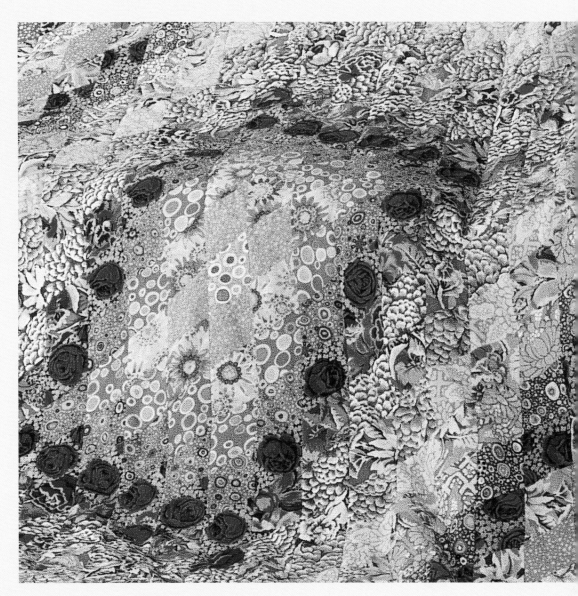

Jubilee Garden by Kaffe Fassett

Orange Grove
by Sandy Donabed

Opposite Easy Peasy cushion (left) and Diagonal Squares cushion (right), this page Blueberry Steps by Kaffe Fassett

ANNA WILLIAMS AND KATHERINE WATTS
A LOUISIANA
QUILTING FRIENDSHIP

by Susan C. Druding – April 2003

At the Houston International Quilt Festival 2000, I found myself returning again and again to view the special exhibit of remarkable quilts by Anna Williams. Previously I had only seen photos of her work and so it was a thrill to see the actual quilts. Recently I was invited to interview Anna Williams and her long time friend Katherine Watts, author of the book *"Anna Williams: her quilts and their influence"*, I eagerly accepted. Meeting them for this article and learning about their long friendship has been a memorable experience.

Above: Anna Williams shows Katherine Watts one of her most recent quilt tops.
Right: detail of quilt XIII from 1990 showing strip piecing built up in log cabin fashion.

This friendship began when these two working mothers met fifty years ago. It is embedded in the American South, where I learned women are respectfully addressed as "Miss". Recently I spent time with Anna Williams and Katherine Watts at their homes in Baton Rouge, Louisiana. These two, born before 1930, each had a mother and a grandmother who quilted and from whom they learned their early quilting skills.

Anna Williams was born in 1927 on a plantation near Baton Rouge and worked there with her family picking crops such as cotton, corn, beans and soybeans. The quilts she made with the women in her family were functional and often made from re-cycled clothing. Miss Anna explained how, as a child, she would pick up little pieces of material to quilt and make doll clothes. After moving to Baton Rouge she began doing housework for various families and in the early 1950s began working for the Watts family and continued with them until her retirement several years ago. In the ensuing years, Miss Anna raised her 8 children and did not have much time to quilt.

Katherine Watts married and had 3 children. Her early interest in sewing and textiles lead her to earn her MA in Home Economics and to teach at Louisiana State University. She introduced a course in surface design and guided many students and her two daughters in the fiber arts. Today her home is filled with a wonderful array of quilts, stitchery and weavings.

While we sat on Miss Anna's porch, the two friends reminisced. Katherine explained how the US Bicentennial in 1976 started a quilting revival. In the late 1970s she, and four partners, opened a shop, "Fiber Five". It became a resource in Baton Rouge for weaving, quilting and textile arts. The shop became a wonderful source of fabrics for Anna Williams, too. Anna chuckled as they talked about her "volunteering" to help at the shop in exchange for fabrics to begin quilting again. By this time in her 50s, Anna began to find her own "voice" in quilting and to develop her unique style. Her quilts were soon to come to the attention of a new generation of art quilters and have a profound effect on their work. Her early quilting experiences in thrifty use of fabric may have played a part in the way she assembled many small pieces into intensely

Above: A strip pieced quilt made in 1995

pieced quilt tops. At first she sewed by hand, assembling long strips while riding the bus and commuting to work in various parts of Baton Rouge and then piecing them together into a whole quilt top. Later, she installed a sewing machine in her bedroom where she still sews today.

Katherine Watts and her daughters first met Nancy Crow, internationally known quilt artist and teacher, in a workshop setting. I asked Nancy Crow to tell me about Katherine Watts, her place in quilt history and in relation to Anna Williams' work.

Nancy Crow:

"Katherine took a class from me at The Arrowmont School of Arts and Crafts in Tennessee in the early 1980's and I was impressed by her knowledge of Central American textiles, her willingness to focus in on quiltmaking, and her general knowledge about how important the contemporary quiltmaking movement was becoming. As I remember she stood out from all the other students because of the above and also because she was one of the few in the class who seemed genuinely interested in quiltmaking as an art form.

We became instant friends and have continued that friendship to this day. Katherine is a very honorable person whose word can be trusted and who has basically given the last 18 years of her life to facilitating the art career of Anna Williams. She became to Anna what Van Gogh's brother was to Van Gogh's life as a painter. Katherine became the lifeline, seeing that there was fabric to be cut up, seeing that the quilt tops were finished, all of which allowed so much more time for Anna to develop and produce ever more work. Katherine found galleries and museums to exhibit Anna's work. She documented her work. She has kept the written history from the first quilts produced by Anna. Katherine is also a heroine for loving Anna enough to give this gift to history."

Katherine found galleries and museums to exhibit Anna's work. She documented her work. She has kept the written history from the first quilts produced by Anna.

How different the art quilt movement would be now if Anna had not showed some of her unique quilt tops to Katherine in the late 1980s. Katherine immediately recognized how extraordinary they were. She showed the quilt tops to Nancy Crow and introduced her to Anna Williams. This lead to a display of Anna Williams' quilt tops at the first Quilt/Surface Design Symposium in 1990 in Columbus, Ohio.

The serious art quilters who attended this Symposium were fascinated - and so Anna Williams' quilts became an inspiration. The term "improvisational quilts" was coined to describe her spontaneous cutting and sewing without the traditional block and template method. Liz Axford, a Houston quilt artist, recalls seeing photos of Anna Williams' quilts taken by friends who attended that first Symposium and being totally bowled over by them as unique in the quilt world.

Liz Axford:

"I had a set of prints [of the photos] made and they stay pinned up on the wall of my studio for years. While I could begin to analyze them and understand how they were put together, I was in total awe of how she conceived of these densely complex surfaces."

I asked Nancy Crow to tell me a little about her perspective on Anna Williams and her quilts and in March 2003, Nancy Crow wrote:

"I believe in Anna and her work because she is an original, she is obsessed and compulsive about making her work

Above: Detail of a quilt formed with triangles and strip-piecing.

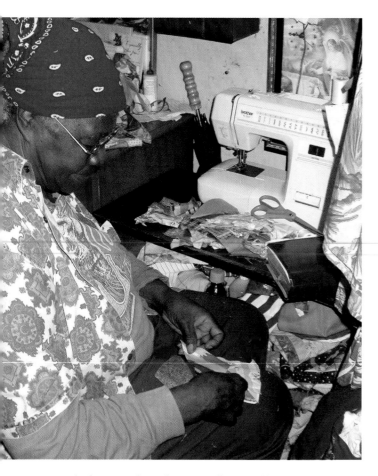

When I talked with Miss Anna about her quilting, I asked her if she began with color ideas or design ideas. She said, "I just think about the patterns, what they will look like and then I get up and lay it out, cut it and then I sew it. Sometimes I sit with my eyes like this (she closed her eyes tightly) and something will come to me and I go through here (she gestured to a large box of fabrics nearby on the floor) and fool with it and then I start … or when I lay in bed some nights I think about it and that's how I got this idea (she indicates the quilt top we are admiring on her bed). I get up and pull the material and look more and take it out until I get it right."

Anna showed me how she sews, cutting triangles with scissors, stacking them on one knee and choosing pairs to put together and sew. She doesn't chain piece, but sews each pair separately and places the finished piece on her other knee. Her sewing machine is in constant use and just came back from the shop. She told me, "The man said that I wore this machine out! Sometimes I sew all day. I just love material!" She patted the area over the feed dogs and said that all the gears had just been replaced. Like all quilters, she has many quilts going at once, and sews on each in turn. She likes to do handwork sitting on her screened-in front porch and has a yo-yo quilt in progress now.

For a number of quilt artists, encountering her work has been a life-altering event. If the measure of an artist is in her or his influence on other artists, as I think it is, then Anna Williams is one of the most important quiltmakers of the 20th century.

which means she is driven......all incredibly important characteristics for true development. Her output has been phenomenal given the fact she did not really begin until she was in her 50s.
Her work is so fresh and so original...all her own even though it shows influences of motifs handed down throughout the history of quiltmaking (just as do the Gee's Bend quilts*). It is her way to putting motifs together that makes her work so distinct and unusual. I like the fact that her work…which can appear incredibly complex….grows out of simplicity; that is, she uses the simplest of means...cotton fabrics, scissors, and a sewing machine....no ruler is used, no templates, no drawings....and all created in a very small room with no wall for pinning up final results. And yet, masterpiece after masterpiece has come out of her production.
She never complains about health problems but rather takes so much pleasure from the fact that she is able to make her quilts. What strength of character this takes...what incredible courage! I admire her so much and hope she will get recognized as one of the great modern quiltmakers she is. She is one of my heroines."

Miss Anna and Miss Katherine formed a company to promote and market Anna Williams' quilts. Anna has always pieced her quilt tops, but didn't want to do the actual quilting and binding of them. Katherine arranged for the quilting and binding by various hand quilters. One of the hand quilters, Mary Walker, enjoys quilting the tops and refers to the process as "settling them down". Over the years, Anna and Katherine have chosen "special" quilts to be in the permanent Anna Williams Collection, now holding over 35 quilts. Katherine has catalogued more than 278 quilt tops completed by Anna since the late 1980s! For those of us who feel we don't have time to quilt, this is an inspiration.

Earlier this year 258,000 people visited Tokyo's International Great Quilt Festival's exhibition, "30 Distinguished Quilt Artists of the World", which included Anna Williams' quilts (her work has been shown in more than 27 exhibits since 1990). The curator, Robert Shaw, not only invited Anna

Above: Anna Williams arranges pairs of triangles on her knee prior to sewing.

Williams to send three quilts, but one of her quilts is on the cover of the catalog for the exhibition.

I asked Robert Shaw to tell me how he views the place Anna Williams holds in the world of quilting. Robert Shaw:

"Re: Anna's place, I would say that she is important both for the quality and originality of her work and for the powerful influence it has had on other quiltmakers. For a number of quilt artists, encountering her work has been a life-altering event. If the measure of an artist is in her or his influence on other artists, as I think it is, then Anna Williams is one of the most important quiltmakers of the 20th century."

The worldwide community of quilters truly has a role model for artistry, inspiration and perseverance in the quilts and person of Anna Williams.

My special gratitude to Katy Prescott for her assistance and to her family for their hospitality during my visit to Baton Rouge.

* Gee's Bend quilts refers to an exhibit of quilts by African-American quilters from Alabama – information: www.tinwoodmedia.com

Bibliography: (partial)

Anna Williams, Her Quilts and their Influence, Watts, Katherine, American Quilt Society, 1995, (out of print).

The Art Quilt, Robert E. Shaw, H. L. Leving Assoc. Pub, 1997

A Different Image: African American Art in Louisiana Collection, catalogue, Arts Council of Greater Baton Rouge, 1997

Contemporary Art Quilts: The John M. Walsh III Collection, University of KY Art Museum, 2001

"30 Distinguished Quilt Artists of the World 2003" catalogue, Tokyo, 2003 (see www.roberteshaw.com for availability)

Links:

www.qsds.com - Quilt Surface Design Symposium

www.nancycrow.com – Nancy Crow's web site

www.roberteshaw.com – Robert Shaw's web site

www.annawilliamsquilts.com - web site featuring Anna Williams' available quilts

www.equilters.com/annawilliams - Susan Druding's web site with photos, bibliography and Anna Williams' exhibits' history.

Comments from quilt artists influenced by Anna Williams will be collected here.

Above: Detail of one of Anna's string pieced quilts made in 1991.

Baby Lozenge Quilt

KAFFE FASSETT

Needlepoint seen in a Washington museum triggered this design. The centres of the 'lozenges' were 'fussy cut' to centre blossoms into a surround of shot cotton.

SIZE OF QUILT
The finished quilt will measure approx. 50in x 45in (127cm x 114cm).

MATERIALS
Patchwork Fabrics:
SHOT COTTON

Opal	SC 05: $^1/4$yd (23cm)
Raspberry	SC 08: $^1/4$yd (23cm)
Tangerine	SC 11: $^1/4$yd (23cm)
Lavender	SC 14: $^1/4$yd (23cm)
Mustard	SC 16: $^1/4$yd (23cm)
Duck Egg	SC 26: $^1/4$yd (23cm)
Mushroom	SC 31: $^1/4$yd (23cm)
Watermelon	SC 33: $^1/4$yd (23cm)
Lilac	SC 36: $^1/4$yd (23cm)
Coffee	SC 37: $^1/4$yd (23cm)
Cobalt	SC 40: $^1/4$yd (23cm)
Lime	SC 43: $^1/4$yd (23cm)

DAMASK

Leafy	GP02-L:	$^1/4$yd (23cm)

FLORAL DANCE

Magenta	GP12-MG:	$^1/4$yd (23cm)
Ochre	GP12-O:	$^1/4$yd (23cm)
Pink	GP12-P:	$^1/4$yd (23cm)

CHRYSANTHEMUM

Blue	GP13-B:	$^1/4$yd (23cm)
Green	GP13-GN:	$^1/4$yd (23cm)

ROWAN STRIPE

RS 01: $^1/4$yd (23cm) or use leftover from backing.

Border Fabrics:
PEONY

Green	GP17-GN:	$^7/8$yd (80cm)

Backing Fabric:
ROWAN STRIPE

RS 01: $2^3/4$yds (2.55m)

Binding Fabric:
ROWAN STRIPE

RS 01: $^1/3$yd (30cm) or use leftover from backing.

Batting:
54in x 49in (137cm x 124.5cm).

Quilting thread:
Toning machine quilting thread

Templates:
see page 94, 98

K   L   M   N   O

PATCH SHAPES
The quilt centre is made up of two row types. The first is made up of two rectangle shapes (templates M & N) which are pieced together with a third rectangle shape (template O) to fill in the extreme ends of the short rows. A triangle shape (template L) is used to piece the second row type along with a second triangle shape (template K) to fill in the extreme ends of these rows.

CUTTING OUT
Template K: Cut $2^5/8$in- (6.75cm-) wide strips across the width of the fabric. Each strip will give you 32 patches per 45in- (114cm-) wide fabric. Cut 20 in RS 01.

Template L: Cut $3^3/8$in- (8.5cm-) wide strips across the width of the fabric. Each strip will give you 26 patches per 45in- (114cm-) wide fabric. Cut 18 in SC 43, 16 in SC 14 & SC 36, 14 in SC 08, SC 26, SC 33, SC 35, SC 40, 12 in SC 05, 10 in SC 11, SC 16, SC 31 & SC 37. For the striped fabric, RS 01 cut $2^3/8$in- (6cm-) wide across the width of the fabric, each strip will give you 23 patches per 45in- (114cm-) wide fabric. Cut 18 in RS 01, this will ensure the stripes are in the correct orientation.

Template M: Cut 3in- (7.5cm-) wide strips across the width of the fabric. Each strip will give you 35 patches per 45in- (114cm-) wide fabric. Cut 18 in SC 43, 16 in SC 14 & SC 36, 14 in SC 08, SC 26, SC 33, SC 35, SC 40, 12 in SC 05, 10 in SC 11, SC 16, SC 31 & SC 37

Template N: Try to cut a blossom centrally in each shape. Cut 17 in GP12-O and GP12-P, 16 in GP12-MG, 14 in GP13-GN, 11 in GP02-L & GP13-B.

Quilt Assembly

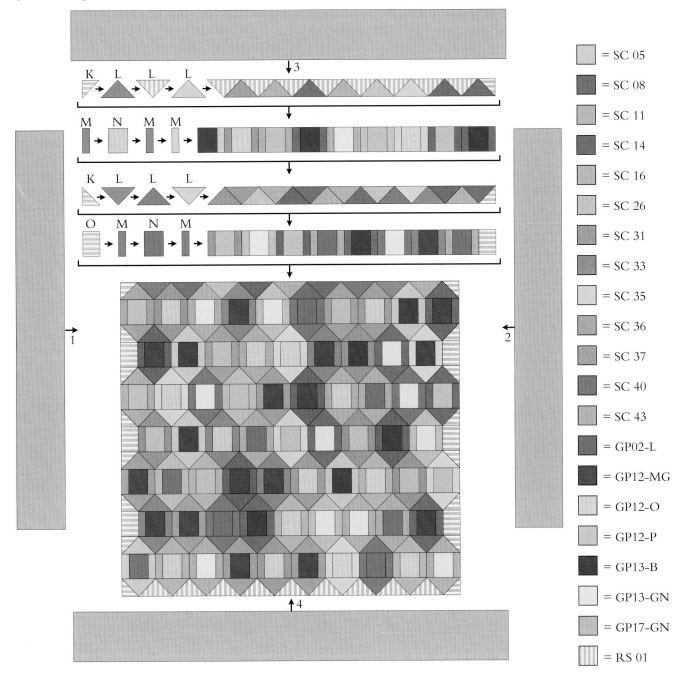

= SC 05
= SC 08
= SC 11
= SC 14
= SC 16
= SC 26
= SC 31
= SC 33
= SC 35
= SC 36
= SC 37
= SC 40
= SC 43
= GP02-L
= GP12-MG
= GP12-O
= GP12-P
= GP13-B
= GP13-GN
= GP17-GN
= RS 01

Template O: Cut 2¹/₄in- (5.75cm-) wide strips across the width of the fabric. Each strip will give you 14 patches per 45in- (114cm-) wide fabric. Cut 8 in RS 01.

Borders: Cut 5 strips 5¹/₂in- (14cm-) wide across the width of the fabric in GP17-GN.

Binding: Cut 5¹/₂yds (5m) of 2¹/₂in- (6.5cm-) wide bias binding from RS 01.

Backing: Cut 1 piece 44in x 49in (112cm x 124.5cm) and 1 piece 11in x 49in (28cm x 124.5cm) in RS 01.

MAKING THE QUILT CENTRE
Using a ¹/₄in (6mm) seam allowance throughout, stitch a total of 19 rows, referring to the quilt assembly diagram for fabric and patch positions.

ADDING THE BORDERS
Join 3 strips to make 1 long strip. From this cut 2 borders each 45¹/₂in by 5¹/₂in (115.5cm x 14cm) for the quilt top and bottom. Trim the 2 remaining strips to 40¹/₂in x 5¹/₂in (103cm x 14cm) for the

quilt sides. Add the borders to the quilt centre in the order indicated by the quilt assembly diagram.

FINISHING THE QUILT
Press the quilt top.
Layer the quilt top, batting and backing and baste together (see page 106). Using a toning machine quilting thread stitch in the ditch along the seam lines or in a loose meandering pattern. Trim the quilt edges and attach the binding (see page 107).

Beyond the Pale Quilt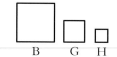

BRANDON MABLY

Backing Fabric:
OMBRE STRIPE

OS 04: $1^1/2$yd (1.4m)

Binding Fabric:
DOTTY

Driftwood   GP14-D: see patchwork
fabrics

Batting:
52in x 44in (132cm x 112cm).

Quilting thread:
Toning machine quilting thread.

Templates:
see page 97, 99

B   G   H

PATCH SHAPES
The quilt centre is made up of two
individual blocks. Block 1 is a four patch
block made from four squares (template G
see page 97). Block 2 is a traditional
Robbing Peter to Pay Paul block, made
from an octagon and four triangles. This
block is made 'the easy way' by using two
sizes of squares (templates B and H see
page 46).

CUTTING OUT
Block 1
Template G: Cut $2^1/2$in- (6.5cm-) wide
strips across the width of the fabric. Each
strip will give you 17 patches per 45in-
(114cm-) wide fabric.
Cut 30 in SC 24, 28 in GP14-L (wrong
side), 20 in GP14-D (wrong side) and
GP14-O (wrong side), 16 in SC 26, SC 36
and GP19-PK, 14 in SC 28.
Block 2
Template B: Cut $4^1/2$in- (11.5cm-) wide
strips across the width of the fabric. Each
strip will give you 9 patches per 45in-
(114cm-) wide fabric.
Cut 11 in GP15-G, 8 in GP01-BW (wrong
side) and GP19-BL, 7 in GP17-BL (wrong
side), 6 in GP17-GR.

Template H: Cut $1^1/2$in- (3.75cm-) wide
strips across the width of the fabric. Each
strip will give you 29 patches per 45in-
(114cm-) wide fabric.
Cut 36 in SC 26, 26 in SC 24 and GP14-O
(wrong side), 24 in SC 36, 22 in SC 05,
18 in SC 28, 8 in SC 14.

B y flipping some fabrics to the 'wrong side' Brandon's quilt has
an almost faded look, cleverly framed by the striped border.

SIZE OF QUILT
The finished quilt will measure approx.
48in x 40in (122cm x 102cm).

MATERIALS
Patchwork Fabrics:
SHOT COTTON

Opal	SC 05:	$1/8$yd (15cm)
Lavender	SC 14:	$1/8$yd (15cm)
Ecru	SC 24:	$1/4$yd (23cm)
Duck Egg	SC 26:	$1/4$yd (23cm)
Blush	SC 28:	$1/4$yd (23cm)
Lilac	SC 36:	$1/4$yd (23cm)

ROMAN GLASS

Blue & White GP01-BW: $1/4$yd (23cm)

DOTTY

Driftwood	GP14-D:	$1/4$yd (23cm)
Lavender	GP14-L:	$1/4$yd (23cm)
Ochre	GP14-O:	$1/4$yd (23cm)

BUBBLES

Grey	GP15-G:	$5/8$yd yd (60cm)

PEONY

Blue	GP17-BL:	$1/4$yd (23cm)
Grey	GP17-GR:	$1/4$yd (23cm)

FRUIT BASKET

Blue	GP19-BL:	$1/4$yd (23cm)
Pink	GP19-PK:	$1/8$yd (15cm)

Border Fabrics:
OMBRE STRIPE

	OS 04:	$1/2$yd (45cm)
	OS 05:	$1/2$yd (45cm)

Quilt Assembly

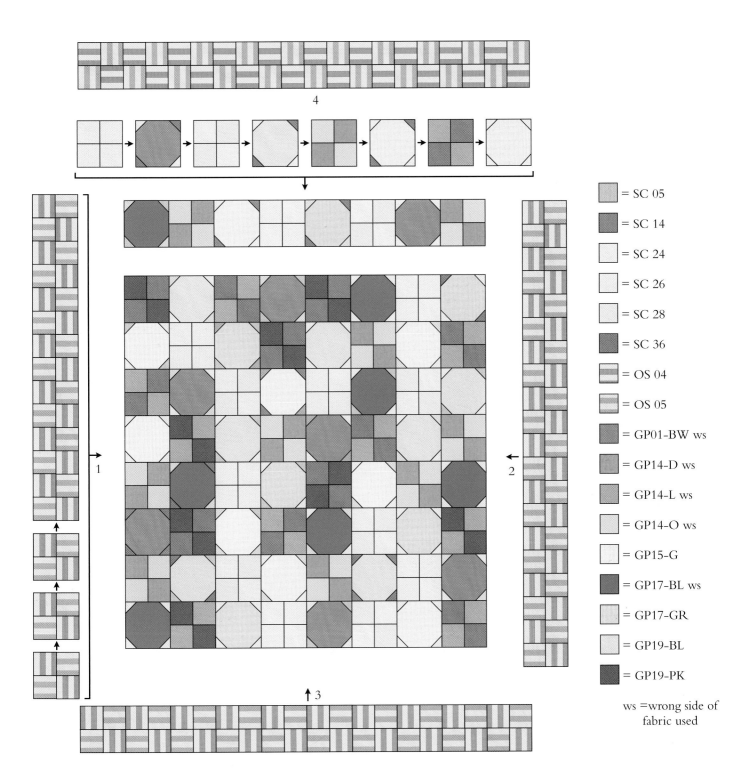

= SC 05
= SC 14
= SC 24
= SC 26
= SC 28
= SC 36
= OS 04
= OS 05
= GP01-BW ws
= GP14-D ws
= GP14-L ws
= GP14-O ws
= GP15-G
= GP17-BL ws
= GP17-GR
= GP19-BL
= GP19-PK

ws =wrong side of fabric used

45

Borders:
Template G: Cut 2¹/₂in- (6.5cm-) wide strips across the width of the fabric. Each strip will give you 17 patches per 45in- (114cm-) wide fabric. Cut 80 in OS 04 and OS 05.
Binding: Cut 5 strips 2in- (5cm-) wide x width of fabric in GP15-G.
Backing: Cut 1 piece 52in x 44in (132cm x 112cm).

MAKING THE BLOCKS

Block 1: Using a ¹/₄in (6mm) seam allowance throughout, using the quilt assembly diagram as a guide to fabric combinations, make a total of 40 blocks for the quilt centre.

Block 2: The technique for making these blocks is simple and quick. Take one large square (template B) and four small squares (template H), using the quilt assembly diagram as a guide to fabric combinations. Place one small square, right sides together onto each corner of the large square, matching the edges carefully as shown in block 2 diagram a. Stitch diagonally across the small squares as shown in diagram b. Trim the corners to a ¹/₄in (6mm) seam allowance and press the corners out (diagram c). Complete 40 blocks for the quilt centre.

MAKING UP THE ROWS

Assemble 10 rows of 8 blocks, use the quilt assembly diagram as a guide.

MAKING THE BORDERS

Make 40 of block 1 from the OS 04 and OS 05 fabrics, using the quilt assembly diagram as a guide to stripe direction. Join the blocks into 4 border lengths, each with 10 blocks and add to the quilt centre in the order indicated by the quilt assembly diagram.

FINISHING THE QUILT

Press the quilt top. Layer the quilt top, batting and backing and baste together (see page 106). Using a toning thread, stitch-in-the-ditch along the seam lines, between the blocks and along each border. Trim the quilt edges and attach the binding (see page 107).

Block Assembly

Block 1 assembly

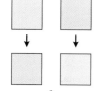

a   b   c

Block 2 assembly

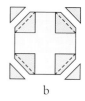

a   b   c

Barcelona Tiles Quilt

MARY MASHUTA

Templates:
see page 94, 97, 102

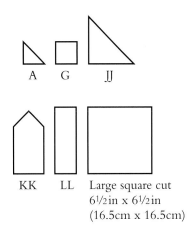

A   G   JJ

KK   LL   Large square cut
6¹/₂in x 6¹/₂in
(16.5cm x 16.5cm)

PATCH SHAPES

The quilt centre is made up of 9 blocks pieced from the following shapes, one large triangle (template JJ), one small triangle (template A), one rectangle (template LL) one small square (template G), one irregular corner shape (template KK) and one large square cut to 6¹/₂in (16.5cm).

The blocks are interspaced with sashing cut to 16¹/₂in x 2¹/₂in (42cm x 6.5cm) and sashing posts (template G) and finished with a simple border.

A trip to Barcelona, Spain, and the work of the architect Antoni Gaudi inspired Mary to design this quilt to showcase Kaffe's mosaic fabrics.

SIZE OF QUILT

The finished quilt will measure approx. 64in x 64in (162.5cm x 162.5cm).

MATERIALS

Patchwork Fabrics:

SHOT COTTON

Pomegranate   SC 09: 1 yd (90cm)

BROAD STRIPE
          BS 08: ¹/₂yd (45cm)

PACHRANGI STRIPE
          PS 05: ³/₄yd (70cm)

ROMAN GLASS
Gold   GP01-G: ¹/₄yd (23cm)

DOTTY
Ochre   GP14-O: ¹/₈yd (15cm) or
            use leftovers from backing.

MOSAIC
Red Gold   GP16-RG: ⁷/₈yd (80cm)
Pink   GP16-PK: ¹/₂yd (45cm)
Purple   GP16-PU: 1¹/₄yds (1.15m)

Backing Fabric:

DOTTY
Ochre   GP14-O: 4 yds (3.7m)

Bias Binding Fabric:

BROAD CHECK
            BC 04: ³/₄yd (70cm)

Batting:
68in x 68in (173cm x 173cm).

Quilting thread:
Maroon and Dark Gold machine quilting thread.

CUTTING OUT

Template A: Cut 2⁷/₈in- (7.25cm-) wide strips across the width of the fabric.
Each strip will give you 28 patches per 45in- (114cm-) wide fabric.
Cut 36 in GP01-G.

Template G: Cut 2¹/₂in- (6.5cm-) wide strip across the width of the fabric.
Cut 16 in GP14-O.

Template JJ: Cut 5¹/₈in- (13cm) wide strips across the width of the fabric.
Each strip will give you 16 patches per 45in- (114cm-) wide fabric.
Cut 72 in GP16-RG and 36 in GP16-PK.

Template KK: Cut 3³/₈in- (13cm) wide strips across the width of the fabric.
Each strip will give you 6 patches per 45in- (114cm-) wide fabric.
Cut 36 in PS 05.

Quilt Assembly

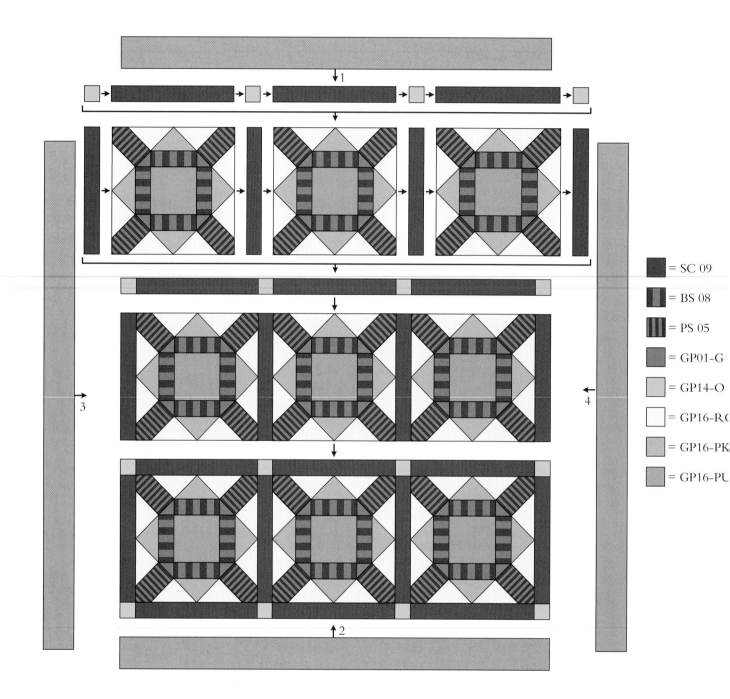

= SC 09

= BS 08

= PS 05

= GP01-G

= GP14-O

= GP16-RC

= GP16-PK

= GP16-PU

Template LL: Cut 2¹/2in- (6.5cm) wide strips across the width of the fabric.
Each strip will give you 6 patches per 45in- (114cm-) wide fabric.
Cut 36 in BS 08.

Large Squares: Cut 6¹/2in- (16.5cm-) wide strips across the width of the fabric. Each strip will give you 6 patches per 45in-

(114cm-) wide fabric. Cut 9 x 6¹/2in (16.5cm) squares in GP16-PU.

Sashing: Cut 16¹/2in- (42cm-) wide strips across the width of the fabric. Each strip will give you 16 patches per 45in- (114cm-) wide fabric. Cut 2¹/2in- (6.5cm-) wide sashing strips down the length of the fabric. Cut a total of 24 sashing strips in SC 09.

Borders: Cut 6 strips 4¹/2in- (11.5cm-) wide x width of fabric in GP16-PU.

Backing: Cut 2 pieces 68in x 45in (173cm by 114cm), and 1 piece 68in x 23¹/2 in (173cm by 60cm) in GP14-O.

Bias Binding: Cut 7¹/2 yds (6.8m) of 2¹/2in- (6.5cm-) wide bias binding from BC 04.

Block Assembly

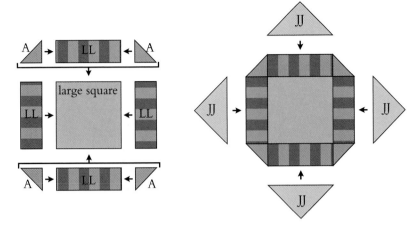

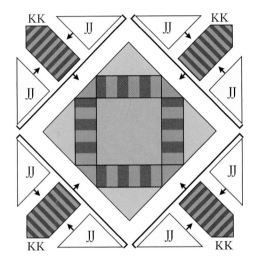

MAKING THE BLOCKS
Using a $1/4$in (6mm) seam allowance throughout, make up 9 blocks, using the block assembly diagrams as a guide.

MAKING THE ROWS
Arrange the blocks and sashing pieces into rows as indicated in the quilt assembly diagram. Join the rows to form the quilt centre.

ADDING THE BORDERS
Join 3 border strips to make 1 long strip. From this cut 2 borders each $56 1/2$in x $4 1/2$in (143.5cm x 11.5cm) for the quilt top and bottom. Join the remaining 3 strips in the same way and from this cut 2 borders each $64 1/2$in x $4 1/2$in (164cm x 11.5cm) for the quilt sides. Add the borders to the quilt centre in the order indicated by the quilt assembly diagram.

FINISHING THE QUILT
Press the quilt top. Seam the backing pieces using a $1/4$in (6mm) seam allowance to form a piece approx. 68in x 68in (173cm x 173cm). Layer the quilt top, batting and backing and baste together (see page 106). Using maroon and dark gold machine quilting thread, quilt as indicated in the quilting diagram. Trim the quilt edges and attach the binding (see page 107).

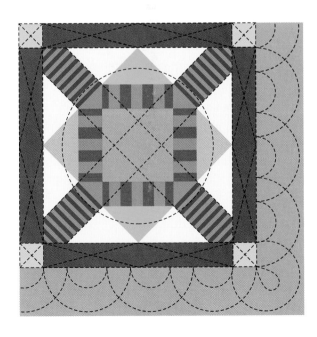

Co-Ordinated Chaos Quilt

SALLY B DAVIS

This is a true scrap quilt with a profusion of wonderful colour combinations. Overall, Sally has used subtle shot cottons with a few checks and many of the stripes in Kaffe's range.
The instructions for this quilt are a little less formal than usual as we have not specified the fabrics, just the total quantities needed.

SIZE OF QUILT
The finished quilt will measure approx. 68in x 82in (173cm x 208cm).

MATERIALS
Patchwork Fabrics:
LIGHT SHOT COTTONS
Include some small quantities of bright 'sharp' contrasting colours to add lift.
Total 2 yds (1.8m)
DARK SHOT COTTONS
Total 2 yds (1.8m)
LIGHT STRIPES
Total: 1¹/4yds (1.15m)

LIGHT CHECKS
Total: ³/4yd (70cm)
DARK STRIPES
Total: 1¹/4yds (1.15m)
DARK CHECKS
Total: ³/4yd (70cm)
Backing Fabric:
FORGET-ME-NOT-ROSE
Jewel   GP08-J: 4 yds (3.7m)
Bias Binding Fabric:
STRIPE OR CHECKED FABRIC
³/4yd (70cm)
Batting:
72in x 86in (183cm x 172cm).

Quilting thread:
Toning machine quilting thread.

Template:
see page 100

MM

PATCH SHAPES
The quilt centre is made up of one rectangular patch shape.

CUTTING OUT
All patches are cut using Template MM:
Light Shot Cottons:
Cut 4¹/2in- (11.5cm-) wide strips across the width of the fabric. Each strip will give you 16 patches per 45in- (114cm-) wide fabric. Cut a total of 175 patches.
Dark Shot Cottons:
Cut 4¹/2in- (11.5cm-) wide strips across the width of the fabric. Each strip will give you 16 patches per 45in- (114cm-) wide fabric. Cut a total of 174 patches.
Light stripes:
To ensure variety of stripe direction cut some 4¹/2in- (11.5cm-) wide strips across the width of the fabric. Each strip will give you 16 patches per 45in- (114cm-) wide fabric, and some 2¹/2in- (6.5cm-) wide strips across the width of the fabric. Each strip will give you 9 patches per 45in- (114cm-) wide fabric. Cut a total of 112 patches.
Light Checks:
Cut 4¹/2in- (11.5cm-) wide strips across the width of the fabric. Each strip will give you 16 patches per 45in- (114cm-) wide fabric. Cut a total of 54 patches.
Dark Stripes:
To ensure variety of stripe direction cut some 4¹/2in- (11.5cm-) wide strips across the width of the fabric. Each strip will give you 16 patches per 45in- (114cm-) wide fabric, and some 2¹/2in- (6.5cm-) wide strips across the width of the fabric. Each strip will give you 9 patches per 45in- (114cm-) wide fabric. Cut a total of 133 patches.
Dark Checks:
Cut 4¹/2in- (11.5cm-) wide strips across the width of the fabric. Each strip will give you 16 patches per 45in- (114cm-) wide fabric. Cut a total of 49 patches.

Quilt Assembly

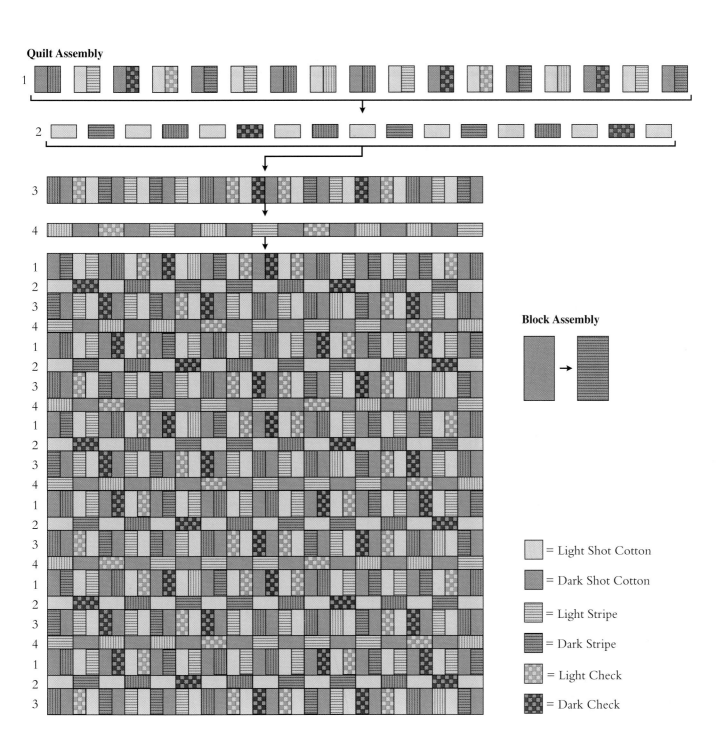

Block Assembly

= Light Shot Cotton

= Dark Shot Cotton

= Light Stripe

= Dark Stripe

= Light Check

= Dark Check

Backing: Cut 2 pieces 72in x 43$^{1}/_{2}$ in (183cm by 114cm) in GP08-J.
Bias Binding: Cut 8$^{3}/_{4}$ yds (8m) of 2$^{1}/_{2}$in- (6.5cm-) wide bias binding.

MAKING THE BLOCKS

Use a $^{1}/_{4}$ in (6mm) seam allowance throughout. Using the block assembly diagrams as a guide, make up 126 'dark' blocks, each 'dark' block has 1 dark shot cotton and 1 dark stripe/check patch, try to choose similar colours/tonal values so that

the finished blocks will read as squares. Make up 112 'light' blocks, each 'light' block has 1 light shot cotton and 1 light stripe/check patch, again choosing similar colours/tonal values.

MAKING THE ROWS

The quilt is made of 4 row types, as shown on the quilt assembly diagram. Make up 7 each of Rows 1, 2 & 3 and 6 of Row 4. Join the rows as indicated in the Quilt assembly diagram.

FINISHING THE QUILT

Press the quilt top. Seam the backing pieces using a $^{1}/_{4}$in (6mm) seam allowance to form a piece approx. 72in x 86in (183cm x 172cm).
Layer the quilt top, batting and backing and baste together (see page 106). Using toning machine quilting thread, quilt a meandering pattern across the surface of the quilt, alternatively stitch-in-the-ditch along the seam lines. Trim the quilt edges and attach the binding (see page 107).

Blueberry Steps

KAFFE FASSETT

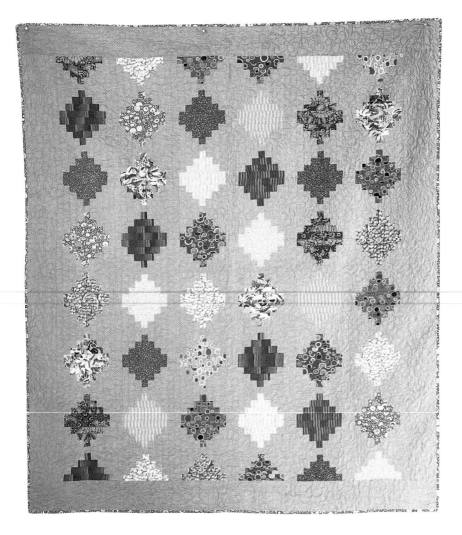

N ow this is made Kaffe wishes he had chosen a different fabric for the border, possibly dotty Lavender.

SIZE OF QUILT

The finished quilt will measure approx. 72in x 63in (183cm x 160cm).

MATERIALS

Patchwork Fabrics:

SHOT COTTON

Mushroom   SC 31: 3¹/₂yds (3.2m)

EXOTIC STRIPE

         ES 15: ¹/₄yd (23cm)

PACHRANGI STRIPE

         PS 01: ¹/₈yd (15cm)

ROWAN STRIPE

         RS 02: ¹/₄yd (23cm)

         RS 05: ¹/₄yd (23cm)

ROMAN GLASS

Blue & White   GP01-BW: ¹/₄yd (23cm)

ARTICHOKES

Circus   GP07-C: ¹/₄yd (23cm)

Pastel   GP07-P: ¹/₄yd (23cm)

FLORAL DANCE

Blue   GP12-B: ¹/₄yd (23cm)

CHRYSANTHEMUM

BLUE   GP13-B: ¹/₄yd (23cm)

DOTTY

Cobalt   GP14-C: ¹/₄yd (23cm)

Sea Green   GP14-SG: ¹/₄yd (23cm)

BUBBLES

Cobalt   GP15-C: ¹/₄yd (23cm)

Plum   GP15-P: ¹/₄yd (23cm)

Sky Blue   GP15-S: ¹/₈yd (15cm)

Border Fabrics:

SHOT COTTON

Mushroom   SC 31: see patchwork fabrics.

Backing Fabric:

SHOT COTTON

Mushroom   SC 31: 3³/₄yds (3.5m)

Binding Fabric:

ROMAN GLASS

Blue & White   GP01-BW: ¹/₂yd (45cm)

Batting:

76in x 67in (193cm x 170cm).

Quilting thread:

Toning machine quilting thread.

Templates:

see page 98

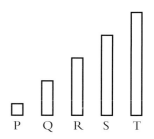

PATCH SHAPES

The quilt centre is comprised of blocks made from one square patch shape (Template P) and four rectangular patch shapes (Templates Q, R, S & T). The blocks are built in layers around a centre square.

CUTTING OUT

Note: Cut in the order specified below for the best use of fabric, i.e. Borders first, then larger patch shapes, always keep the leftovers and use for the smaller sizes.

Borders: Cut from the length of the fabric 4 strips 4¹/₂in x 65in (11.5cm x 165cm) in SC 31. Trim to fit exactly once the quilt centre is finished as described below. Use the remaining fabric to cut Template T and further patch shapes as described below.

Template T: Cut 1¹/₂in- (3.75cm-) wide strips across the width of the fabric. Each strip will give you 4 patches per 45in- (114cm-) wide fabric. Cut 84 in SC 31.

Quilt Assembly

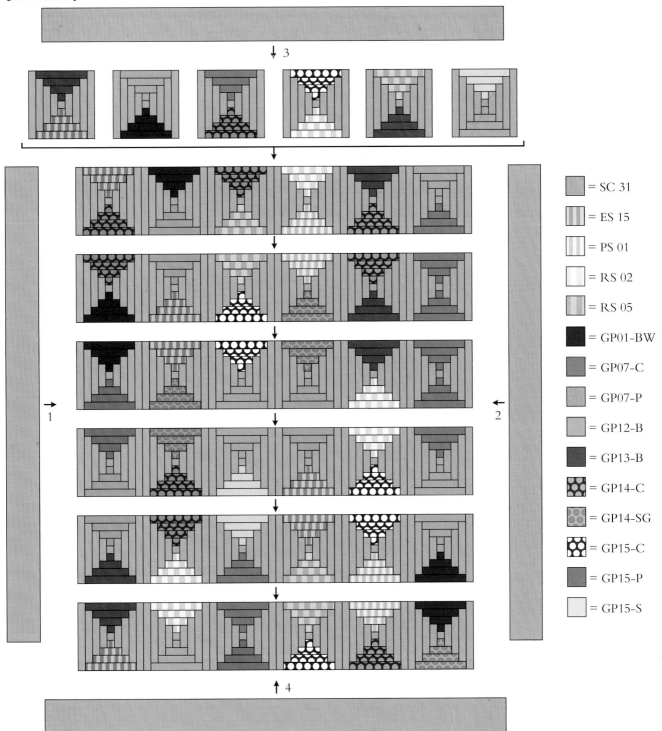

Legend:
- = SC 31
- = ES 15
- = PS 01
- = RS 02
- = RS 05
- = GP01–BW
- = GP07–C
- = GP07–P
- = GP12–B
- = GP13–B
- = GP14–C
- = GP14–SG
- = GP15–C
- = GP15–P
- = GP15–S

Template S: Cut 1¹/₂in- (3.75cm-) wide strips across the width of the fabric.
Each strip will give you 5 patches per 45in- (114cm-) wide fabric. Cut 84 in SC 31, 9 in GP14-C, 8 in GP12-B, 7 in ES 15, GP13-B, GP15-P, 6 in RS 02, GP01-BW, GP07-P, GP15-C, 5 in RS 05, GP07-C, GP14-SG, 4 in PS 01 and 3 in GP15-S.

Template R: Cut 1¹/₂in- (3.75cm-) wide strips across the width of the fabric.
Each strip will give you 8 patches per 45in- (114cm-) wide fabric. Cut 84 in SC 31, 9 in GP14-C, 8 in GP12-B, 7 in ES 15, GP13-B, GP15-P, 6 in RS 02, GP01-BW, GP07-P, GP15-C, 5 in RS 05, GP07-C, GP14-SG, 4 in PS 01 and 3 in GP15-S.

Template Q: Cut 1¹/₂in- (3.75cm-) wide strips across the width of the fabric.
Each strip will give you 12 patches per 45in- (114cm-) wide fabric. Cut 84 in SC 31, 9 in GP14-C, 8 in GP12-B, 7 in ES 15, GP13-B, GP15-P, 6 in RS 02, GP01-BW, GP07-P, GP15-C, 5 in RS 05, GP07-C, GP14-SG, 4 in PS 01 and 3 in GP15-S.

Chintz Flowerbeds Quilt 🧵🧵

KAFFE FASSETT

Block Assembly (Diagram A)

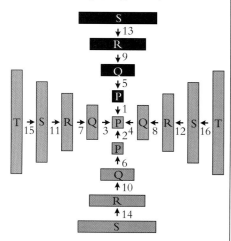

Template P: Cut 1^1/2in- (3.75cm-) wide strips across the width of the fabric. Each strip will give you 29 patches per 45in- (114cm-) wide fabric. Cut 42 in SC 31, 9 in GP14-C, 8 in GP12-B, 7 in ES 15, GP13-B, GP15-P, 6 in RS 02, GP01-BW, GP07-P, GP15-C, 5 in RS 05, GP07-C, GP14-SG, 4 in PS 01 and 3 in GP15-S.

Backing: Cut 1 piece 67in x 45in (170cm x 114cm) and 1 piece 67in x 31^1/2in (170cm x 80cm) in SC 31.

Binding: Cut 7 strips 2in- (5cm-) wide x width of fabric in GP01-BW

MAKING THE BLOCKS

Using a ^{1}/4in (6mm) seam allowance throughout, referring to the quilt assembly diagram for fabric combinations, make 48 blocks by following the sequence shown in diagram A.

MAKING UP THE ROWS

Assemble the quilt into 7 rows of 6 blocks as shown in the quilt assembly diagram. Join the rows to form the quilt centre.

ADDING THE BORDERS

Trim the side borders to fit and stitch in place, then trim the top and bottom borders and stitch as indicated by the quilt assembly diagram.

FINISHING THE QUILT

Press the quilt top. Layer the quilt top, batting and backing and baste together (see page 106). Using a toning machine quilting thread, stitch a loose meandering pattern across the surface of the quilt. Trim the quilt edges and attach the binding (see page 107).

A n exciting showcase for Kaffe's August Rose fabrics.

SIZE OF QUILT

The finished quilt will measure approx. 94in x 94in (239cm x 239cm).

MATERIALS

Patchwork Fabrics:

ROMAN GLASS

Red	GP01-R:	2^1/4yds (2.10m)

DAMASK

Jewel	GP02-J:	1^1/4yd (1.15m)

FLOWER LATTICE

Jewel	GP11-J:	1^1/4yd (1.15m)

FLORAL DANCE

Magenta	GP12-MG:	2^1/2yds (2.3m) or use leftover from backing and buy 1^1/4yds (1.15m)
Pink	GP12-P:	^{3}/4yd (70cm)

AUGUST ROSES

Magenta	GP18-MG:	^{1}/2yd (45cm)
Ochre	GP18-OC:	1^1/4yd (1.15m)
Pink	GP18-PK:	^{3}/4yd (70cm)
Purple	GP18-PU:	^{1}/2yd (45cm)

Suffolk Puff Fabrics:

SHOT COTTON

Watermelon	SC 33:	^{1}/4yd (23cm)
Jade	SC 41:	^{1}/2yd (45cm)

Backing Fabric:

FLORAL DANCE

Magenta	GP12-MG:	8^1/2yds (7.8m)

Binding Fabric:

ROMAN GLASS

Red	GP01-R:	see patchwork fabrics

Batting:
100in x 100in (254cm x 254cm).

Quilting thread:
Toning machine quilting thread and fine Coats perlé thread in maroon and salmon pink.

Quilt Assembly

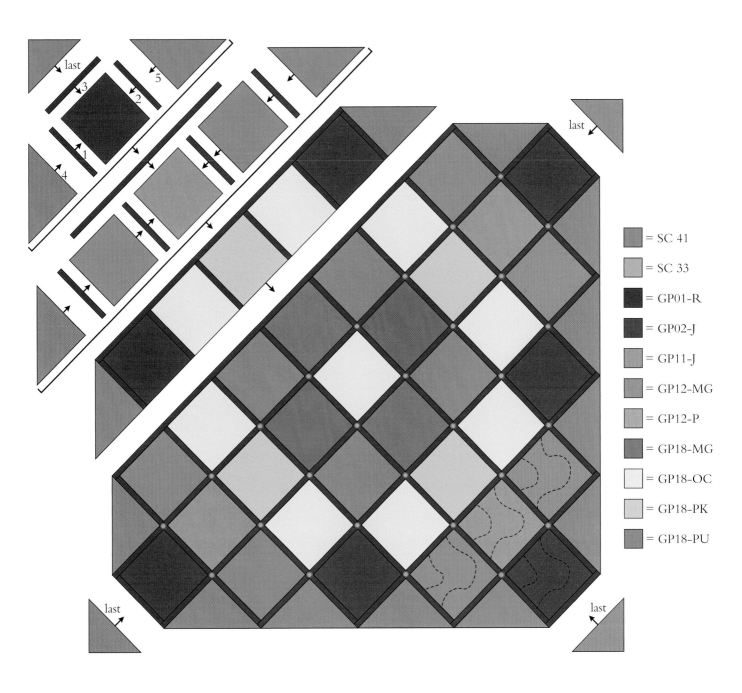

= SC 41
= SC 33
= GP01-R
= GP02-J
= GP11-J
= GP12-MG
= GP12-P
= GP18-MG
= GP18-OC
= GP18-PK
= GP18-PU

Templates:
see page 96

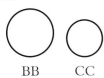

BB   CC

PATCH SHAPES

The quilt is made up of one large square patch shape (see diagram a), interspaced with sashing.

The quilt edges are filled in using a triangle patch shape (see diagram b) and the extreme corners with a second triangle patch shape (see diagram c), these are cut oversize and trimmed to the correct size after stitching.

It is finished with a wider than usual binding and is embellished with Suffolk Puffs (see glossary).

CUTTING OUT

Centre squares: Cut $12^1/2$in- (31.75cm-) wide strips across the width of the fabric. Each strip will give you 3 patches per 45in- (114cm-) wide fabric.

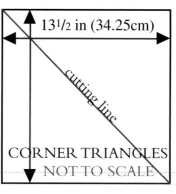

a

Cut 9 in GP18-OC, 8 in GP02-J, GP11-J, 4 in GP12-P, GP12-MG, GP18-PK, 2 in GP18-MG and GP18-PU.

Side triangles: Cut 2 x $22^1/4$in- (56.5cm-) wide strips across the width of the fabric. Each strip will give you 8 patches per 45in- (114cm-) wide fabric. Cut 4 x $22^1/4$in (56.5cm) squares in GP12-MG. Using diagram b as a guide cut each square in half diagonally and without moving the pieces cut again across the opposite diagonal to make 4 triangles.

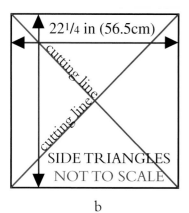

b

Corner triangles: Cut $13^1/2$in- (34.25cm-) wide strips across the width of the fabric. Cut 2 x $13^1/2$in (34.25cm) squares in GP12-MG. Cut once diagonally as shown in diagram c to make 4 corner triangles.

c

Sashing: Cut a total of 33 x $1^1/2$in- (3.75cm-) wide strips across the width of the fabric. From these cut 50 sashing strips $1^1/2$in x $12^1/2$in (3.75cm x 31.75cm). The remaining strips will be used for the longer sashing lengths as detailed below.
Template BB: Cut 40 in SC 41.
Template CC: Cut 40 in SC 33.
Binding: Cut 9 strips 3in- (7.5m-) wide x width of fabric in GP01-R.
Backing: Cut 2 pieces 100in x 45in (254cm x 114cm) and 1 piece 100in x 11in (254cm x 28cm) in GP12-MG.

MAKING THE QUILT

Using a $1/4$in (6mm) seam allowance throughout, make 2 sashing strips in each of the following lengths: $1^1/2$in x $14^1/2$in

(3.75cm x 36.75cm), $1^1/2$in x $40^1/2$in (3.75cm x 103cm), $1^1/2$in x $66^1/2$in (3.75cm x 169cm), $1^1/2$in x $92^1/2$in (3.75cm x 235cm) and $1^1/2$in x $118^1/2$in (3.75cm x 301cm). Lay out the $12^1/2$in (31.75cm) squares in the sequence indicated in the quilt assembly diagram, separating the squares with $1^1/2$in x $12^1/2$in (3.75cm x 31.75cm) sashing strips. Join into diagonal rows, interspacing the rows with the longer sashing strips, finally add the corner triangles.

MAKING THE SUFFOLK PUFFS

Turn under a $1/4$in (6mm) hem of each fabric circle and sew a running stitch using strong thread around the outer edge. Making sure the right side of the fabric is the outside of the Puff, gently pull the thread, gathering the fabric until a small opening is left. Knot the thread. Make 40 in each colour way. Layer the smaller on top of the larger and stitch at the sashing intersections as shown in the quilt assembly diagram.

FINISHING THE QUILT

Press the quilt top. Seam the backing pieces using a $1/4$in (6mm) seam allowance to form a piece approx. 100in x 100in (254cm x 254cm).

Layer the quilt top, batting and backing and baste together (see page 106). Using a toning thread, machine stitch-in-the-ditch along the seam lines, Also hand quilt a random curve pattern as indicated in the bottom right section of the quilt assembly diagram. Trim the quilt edges $1/2$in (1.25cm) beyond the points of the sashing, attach the binding with a $1/2$in (1.25cm) seam allowance (see page 107).

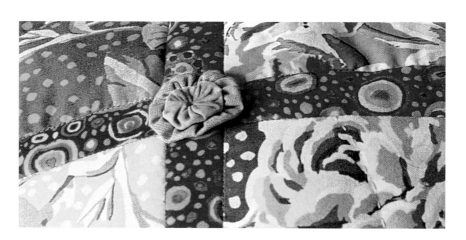

Extended Pinwheels Quilt

KAFFE FASSETT

Grass	SC 27:	$^1/_8$yd (15cm)
Cobalt	SC 40:	$^1/_4$yd (23cm)
Jade	SC 41:	$^1/_4$yd (23cm)
BROAD CHECK		
	BC 02:	$^1/_8$yd (15cm)
EXOTIC STRIPE		
	ES 15:	$^3/_4$yd (70cm)
	ES 16:	$^1/_4$yd (23cm)
NARROW CHECK		
	NC 02:	$^1/_4$yd (23cm)
PACHRANGI STRIPE		
	PS 01:	$^5/_8$yd (60cm)
DOTTY		
Cobalt	GP14-C:	$^5/_8$yd (60cm)
Plum	GP14-P:	$^1/_3$yd (30cm)

Inner Border Fabrics:
DOTTY
Cobalt   GP14-C: see patchwork fabrics

Middle Border Fabrics:
EXOTIC STRIPE
              ES 15: see patchwork fabrics

Outer Border Fabrics:
BROAD STRIPE
              BS 23: $^1/_3$yd (30cm)

Backing Fabric:
NARROW CHECK
              NC 02: 2 yd (1.85m)

Binding Fabric:
PACHRANGI STRIPE
              PS 01: see patchwork fabrics

Batting:
58in x 50in (148cm x 127cm).

Quilting thread:
Toning machine quilting thread.

Template:
see page 94

TThe vigour of exploding pinwheels is an exciting structure for this Islamic blue palette. The rag rug was specially made to go with the quilt.

SIZE OF QUILT
The finished quilt will measure approx. 54in x 46in (137cm x 117cm).

MATERIALS
Patchwork Fabrics:
SHOT COTTON
Cassis   SC 02: $^1/_8$yd (15cm)

Prune	SC 03:	$^1/_8$yd (15cm)
Opal	SC 05:	$^1/_4$yd (23cm)
Chartreuse	SC 12:	$^1/_8$yd (15cm)
Lavender	SC 14:	$^1/_4$yd (23cm)
Denim	SC 15:	$^1/_4$yd (23cm)
Smoky	SC 20:	$^1/_4$yd (23cm)
Pine	SC 21:	$^1/_3$yd (30cm)
Pewter	SC 22:	$^1/_8$yd (15cm)

A

PATCH SHAPES
The quilt centre is made up from a single triangle patch (template A)

Quilt Assembly

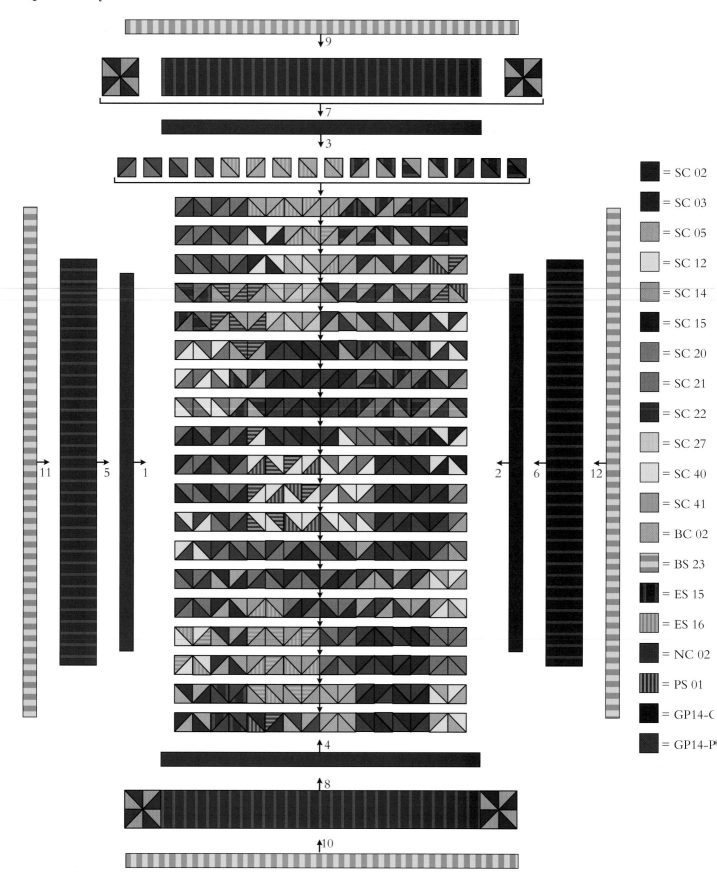

= SC 02
= SC 03
= SC 05
= SC 12
= SC 14
= SC 15
= SC 20
= SC 21
= SC 22
= SC 27
= SC 40
= SC 41
= BC 02
= BS 23
= ES 15
= ES 16
= NC 02
= PS 01
= GP14-C
= GP14-P

58

CUTTING OUT

Template A: Cut $2^7/8$in- (7.25cm-) wide strips across the width of the fabric. Each strip will give you 28 patches per 45in- (114cm-) wide fabric.

Cut 4 in SC 02, 18 in SC 03, 47 in SC 05, 19 in SC 12, 37 in SC 14, 30 in SC 15 (includes 16 for middle borders), 48 in SC 20, 60 in SC 21, 18 in SC 22, 8 in SC 27, 41 in SC 40, 42 in SC 41 (includes 16 for middle borders), 20 in BC 02, 46 in ES 15, 32 in ES 16, 42 in NC 02, 27 in PS 01, 76 in GP14-C, 57 in GP14-P.

Inner Borders: For side borders cut 2 strips $40^1/2$in x 2in (103cm x 5cm) and for top and bottom borders cut 2 strips $35^1/2$in x 2in (90cm x 5cm) in GP14-C.

Middle Borders: For side borders cut 2 strips $43^1/2$in x $5^1/2$in (110.5cm x 14cm) and for top and bottom borders cut 2 strips $35^1/2$in x $4^1/2$in (90cm x 14cm) in ES 15. You will also need the 16 triangles in SC 15 and 16 triangles in SC 41 as specified above.

Outer Borders: For top and bottom borders cut 2 strips $43^1/2$in x 2in (110.5cm x 5cm) and for side borders cut

3 strips 2 in (5cm) x the width of the fabric, join into 1 length and from this cut 2 strips $54^1/2$in x 2in (138.5cm x 5cm) in BS 23.

Binding: Cut 6 yards of bias binding $2^1/2$in- (5cm-) wide from PS 01.

Backing: Cut 1 piece 58in x 45in (147cm by 114cm) and 2 pieces 29in x 6in (58cm by 15.5cm) in NC 02.

MAKING THE BLOCKS

Using a $^1/4$in (6mm) seam allowance throughout, make up 320 blocks, use the quilt and block assembly diagrams as a guide. Also make up 16 blocks for the middle border corner sections.

Block Assembly

MAKING UP THE ROWS

Assemble 20 rows of 16 blocks, use the quilt assembly diagram as a guide.

MAKING THE BORDERS

Add the inner borders to the quilt centre in the order indicated by the quilt assembly diagram. Add the side middle borders to the quilt centre. Join the 16 corner section blocks into 4 square pinwheels, add one to each end of the top and bottom middle borders and add to quilt centre. Add outer borders to the quilt centre in the order indicated by the quilt assembly diagram.

FINISHING THE QUILT

Press the quilt top. Seam the backing pieces using a $^1/4$in (6mm) seam allowance to form a piece approx. 58in x 50in (147cm by 127cm). Layer the quilt top, batting and backing and baste together (see page 106). Using a toning thread, stitch-in-the-ditch along the seam lines, between the blocks and along each border. Trim the quilt edges and attach the binding (see page 107).

Fiesta Quilt

KAFFE FASSETT

T The dramatic zigzags in this quilt are accentuated by the black pointed rooflines of the net drying sheds in Hastings. You could add leftovers from other Rowan projects to the fabrics Kaffe chose.

SIZE OF QUILT
The finished quilt will measure approx. 91in x 71in (234cm x 180cm).

MATERIALS
Patchwork Fabrics:
SHOT COTTON

Ginger	SC 01:	1/4yd (23cm)
Persimmon	SC 07:	3/4yd (70cm)
Raspberry	SC 08:	3/4yd (70cm)
Pomegranate	SC 09:	3/4yd (70cm)
Bittersweet	SC 10:	3/4yd (70cm)
Tangerine	SC 11:	3/4yd (70cm)
Chartreuse	SC 12:	1/2yd (45cm)
Lavender	SC 14:	1/2yd (45cm)
Mustard	SC 16:	1/8yd (15cm)
Duck Egg	SC 26:	1/2yd (45cm)
Rosy	SC 32:	1/2yd (45cm)
Watermelon	SC 33:	1/2yd (45cm)

ALTERNATE STRIPE

	AS 10:	1/2yd (45cm)

BROAD STRIPE

	BS 11:	1/2yd (45cm)

BLUE AND WHITE STRIPE

	BWS02:	1/4yd (23cm)

NARROW STRIPE

	NS 01:	1/4yd (23cm)
	NS 16:	1/4yd (23cm)

ROWAN STRIPE

	RS 04:	1/8yd (15cm)
	RS 05:	1/8yd (15cm)
	RS 07:	1/8yd (15cm)

ROMAN GLASS

Circus	GP01-C:	1/8yd (15cm)
Gold	GP01-G:	1/2yd (45cm)
Jewel	GP01-J:	1/8yd (15cm)
Pink	GP01-PK:	1/8yd (15cm)
Red	GP01-R:	1/4yd (23cm)

ARTICHOKES

Jewel	GP07-J:	1/4yd (23cm) or use leftovers from backing.

FORGET-ME-NOT ROSE

Jewel	GP08-J:	1/8yd (15cm)

CHRYSANTHEMUM

Red	GP13-R:	3/4yd (70cm)

DOTTY

Driftwood	GP14-D:	1/8yd (15cm)

BUBBLES

Ochre	GP15-O:	1/8yd (15cm)
Plum	GP15-P:	1/8yd (15cm)

Border Fabrics:
A selection of leftovers from the patchwork fabrics

Backing Fabric:
ARTICHOKES

Jewel	GP07-J:	51/2yd (5.1m)

Binding Fabric:
A selection of leftovers from the patchwork fabrics

Batting:
96in x 75in (244cm x 191cm).

Quilting thread:
Perle cotton thread in bright colours.

Template:
see page 94

J

Quilt Assembly

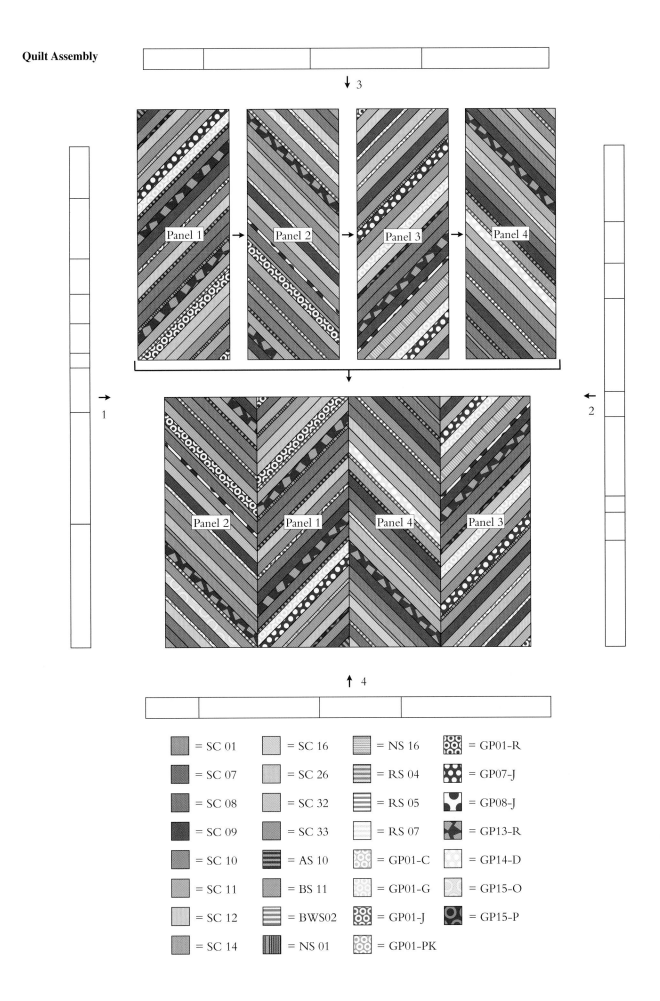

	= SC 01		= SC 16		= NS 16		= GP01-R
	= SC 07		= SC 26		= RS 04		= GP07-J
	= SC 08		= SC 32		= RS 05		= GP08-J
	= SC 09		= SC 33		= RS 07		= GP13-R
	= SC 10		= AS 10		= GP01-C		= GP14-D
	= SC 11		= BS 11		= GP01-G		= GP15-O
	= SC 12		= BWS02		= GP01-J		= GP15-P
	= SC 14		= NS 01		= GP01-PK		

Block Assembly

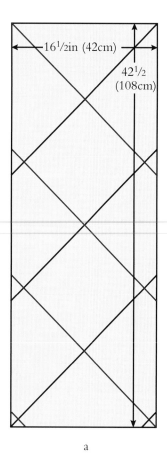

16¹/₂in (42cm)

42¹/₂ (108cm)

a

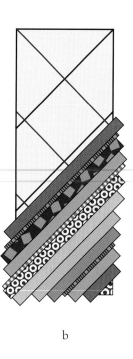

b

PATCH SHAPES

The quilt centre is made up of 4 panels, each repeated once to make a total of 8 panels. They are pieced using two strip sizes starting from one corner triangle for which a template is provided to 'set' the correct 45 degree angle (template J see page 94).

CUTTING OUT

Template J: Cut 2 in SC 08, SC 14, SC 26 and GP01-R.

Borders: Cut a selection of 4in- (10cm-) wide strips parallel to the selvedge of the patchwork fabrics. Leave on one side.

Panels: The following is just a guide, you may need to cut extra strips, but don't cut

them until you need them. Use the off cuts as you go along for the shorter corner lengths join them for longer lengths where necessary. Cut strips across the width of the fabric EXCEPT in the case of SC 07, SC 09, SC 11, SC 08, SC 10 and GP13-R cut these down the length of the fabric.

2in (5cm) Strips: Cut 14 in SC 11, 12 in SC 07, SC 09, 10 in SC 08, SC 10, GP13-R, 8 in SC 33, 4 in SC 12, SC 14, SC 26, SC 32, GP01-G, GP01-R, GP07-J, 2 in SC 01, NS 16, GP14-D, 1 in SC 16, GP15-O.

1in (2.5cm) Strips: Cut 6 in AS 10, 4 in BS 11, BWS02, NS 01, GP08-J, 2 in NS 16, RS 04, RS 05, RS 07, GP01-C, GP01-J, GP01-PK, GP15-P.

Binding: Cut a selection of 2in- (5cm-) wide strips from the patchwork fabric leftovers. Cut the strips into random length rectangles. Stitch into one long length until you have 9¹/₂ yards (8.75m) of binding.

Backing: Cut 1 piece 96in x 44in (240cm x 112cm) and 1 piece 96in x 32in (240cm x 81cm) in GP07-J

MAKING THE PANELS

The panels are pieced using a paper guide, using a ¹/₄in (6mm) seam allowance throughout. This is not quite the same as foundation piecing as the fabric is not stitched to the paper, but the principle is the same. Make a paper guide 16¹/₂in x

42$^{1}/_{2}$in (42cm x 108cm). Mark the paper with 45 degree diagonal lines as shown in diagram a. See page 62. The blue lines are the guide for panels 1 and 3, (start piecing from the bottom right corner) and the red lines are the guide for panels 2 and 4 (start piecing from the bottom left corner). Referring to the quilt assembly diagram for fabric placement, take the cut triangle template J match it carefully onto the paper guide and place the next fabric strip right sides together on the triangle. Pin along the stitching line and flip back to ensure that the strip overlaps and completely covers the edge of the paper. Stitch the strip into place and press very carefully. Add the next strip in the same manner. Each time a new strip is added, press carefully and check that the panel covers the guide and that the angle is still at 45 degree as shown in diagram b. See page 62.

When the guide is completely covered, match the corner triangle to the guide edge and trim the panel to fit the guide exactly.

MAKING UP THE ROWS

Join the panels into 2 rows of 4 panels, referring to the quilt assembly diagram for placement. Join the rows to form the quilt centre.

MAKING THE BORDERS

Take the 4in- (10cm-) wide strips and lay them around your quilt centre in a pleasing arrangement, cutting the strips into random length rectangles as you please. Stitch 2 borders 4in x 84$^{1}/_{2}$in (10cm x 214.5cm) and add to the quilt sides. Stitch 2 borders 4in x 71$^{1}/_{2}$in (10cm x 181.5cm) and add to the quilt top and bottom.

FINISHING THE QUILT

Press the quilt top.

Layer the quilt top, batting and backing and baste together (see page 106).

Using bright hand quilting threads and bold stitching, quilt lines offset about $^{1}/_{4}$in (6mm) from the seam lines on the wider strips.

Trim the quilt edges and attach the binding (see page 107).

Fizz Quilt

PAULINE SMITH

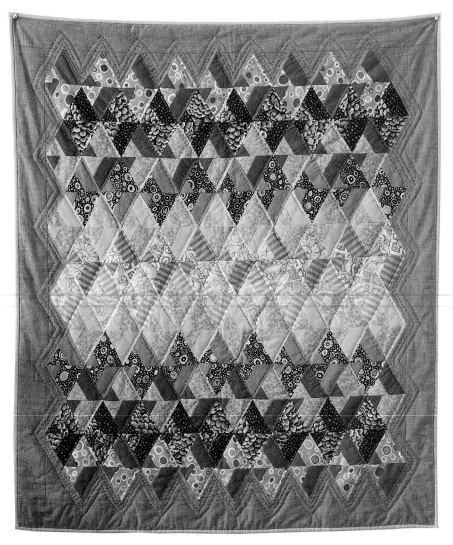

The fabric quantities on this quilt work to within a hairs breadth, so if you are a novice, then we suggest you buy a little more!

Backing Fabric:
ROWAN STRIPE
RS 02: 1¹/2yd (1.4m)

Binding Fabric:
SHOT COTTON
Apple   SC 39: see patchwork
                 fabrics

Batting:
51¹/2in x 45in (131cm x 114cm).

Quilting thread:
Variegated hand quilting thread in bright colours.

Templates:
see page 94, 96

△   △   ◁
D   E   F

PATCH SHAPES

The quilt centre is made up of one triangle patch shape (Template D). Using this shape patches are cut from strips which have been seamed together. Two additional triangle shapes are used to fill the edges of the quilt (Templates E & F).

CUTTING OUT

Template D: Two strip widths are required. These are then seamed together and the triangles are cut from the resulting fabric (see page 65 for more details).
Cut 2¹/2in- (6.5cm-) wide strips across the width of the fabric.
Cut 4 strips in GP14-SG, 2 strips in GP01-BW, GP07-C, and GP15-G, 1 strip in GP13-GN and GP13-O
Cut 2in- (5cm-) wide strips across the width of the fabric.
Cut 2 strips in SC 05, SC 14, SC 39, SC 40 and GP14-C, 1 strip in RS 02 and RS 07.
For the plain setting triangles on the quilt top and bottom, cut 4in- (10cm-) wide strips across the width of the fabric. Each strip will give you 18 patches per 45in- (114cm-) wide fabric. Cut 18 in SC 36.
Template E: Cut 2⁵/8in- (6.75cm-) wide strips across the width of the fabric.
Cut 2 in SC 36.

SIZE OF QUILT

The finished quilt will measure approx. 48¹/4in x 41¹/2in (122.5cm x 105.5cm).

MATERIALS

Patchwork Fabrics:
SHOT COTTON

Opal	SC 05:	¹/4yd (23cm)
Lavender	SC 14:	¹/4yd (23cm)
Lilac	SC 36:	³/4yd (70cm)
Apple	SC 39:	¹/2yd (45cm)
Cobalt	SC 40:	¹/4yd (23cm)

ROMAN GLASS
Blue & White GP01-BW: ¹/4yd (23cm)
ARTICHOKES
Circus   GP07-C: ¹/4yd (23cm)

CHRYSANTHEMUM

Green	GP13-GN:	¹/8yd (15cm)
Ochre	GP13-O:	¹/8yd (15cm)

DOTTY

Cobalt	GP14-C:	¹/4yd (23cm)
Sea Green	GP14-SG:	⁵/8yd (60cm)

BUBBLES
Grey   GP15-G: ¹/4yd (23cm)
ROWAN STRIPE
              RS 02: ¹/8yd (15cm) or
              use excess from backing.
              RS 07: ¹/8yd (15cm)

Border Fabrics:
SHOT COTTON
Lilac   SC 36: see patchwork
              fabrics

Quilt Assembly

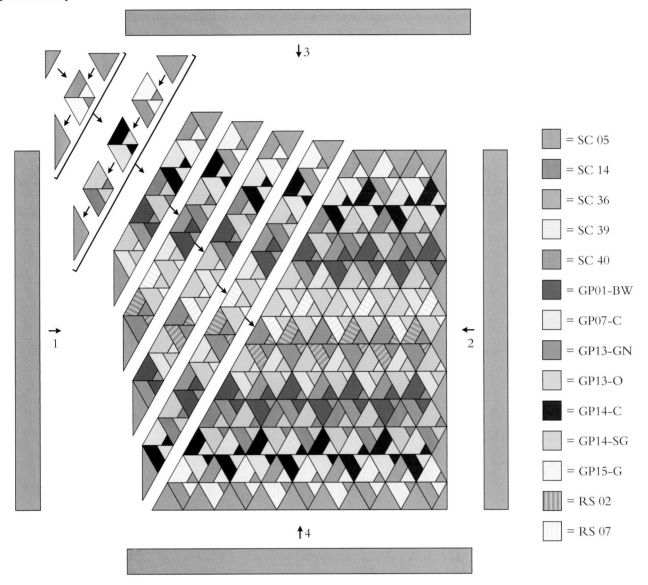

= SC 05
= SC 14
= SC 36
= SC 39
= SC 40
= GP01-BW
= GP07-C
= GP13-GN
= GP13-O
= GP14-C
= GP14-SG
= GP15-G
= RS 02
= RS 07

Template F: Cut 2¹/₂in- (6.5cm-) wide strips across the width of the fabric. Each strip will give you 9 patches per 45in- (114cm-) wide fabric. Cut 12 in SC 36.

Borders: Cut 4 strips 3¹/₂in- (9cm-) wide across the width of the fabric in SC 36. Trim to fit once the quilt centre is finished as described below.

Binding: Cut 6 strips 2in- (5cm-) wide x width of fabric in SC 39.

Backing: Cut 1 piece 51¹/₂in x 45in (131cm x 114cm) in RS 02.

MAKING THE BLOCKS

Using a ¹/₄in (6mm) seam allowance throughout, referring to the quilt assembly diagram for fabric combinations, stitch sets of 2in (5cm) and 2¹/₂in (6.5cm) strips together as shown in block diagram a. Using template D, cut triangles by rotating the template. Take consecutive pairs of triangles as shown in diagram b, rotate them and stitch them as shown in diagram c, to make two types of block as shown in diagram d.

Quilting Diagram

Block Assembly

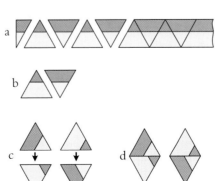

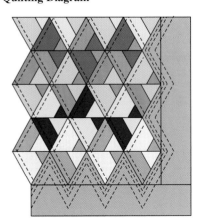

65

MAKING UP THE ROWS

Assemble the quilt into diagonal rows as shown in the quilt assembly diagram, using the plain triangles in SC 36 (templates D, E & F) to fill in along edges.

ADDING THE BORDERS

Trim the side borders to fit and stitch in place, then trim the top and bottom borders and stitch as indicated by the quilt assembly diagram.

FINISHING THE QUILT

Press the quilt top. Layer the quilt top, batting and backing and baste together (see page 106). Using a bright variegated hand quilting thread, quilt as indicated in the quilting diagram. Trim the quilt edges and attach the binding (see page 107).

Musetta Quilt

LIZA PRIOR LUCY

B izet's Opera, Carmen, and in particular the 'hot babe' Musetta, were the sparks which ignited Liza's imagination.

SIZE OF QUILT

The finished quilt will measure approx. 73³/₄in x 73³/₄in (187.5cm x 187.5cm).

MATERIALS

Patchwork Fabrics:

SHOT COTTON
Cassis	SC 02:	¹/₈yd (15cm)
Chartreuse	SC 12:	¹/₄yd (23cm)
Lavender	SC 14:	¹/₈yd (15cm)
Denim	SC 15:	¹/₈yd (15cm)
Mushroom	SC 31:	¹/₈yd (15cm)

NARROW STRIPE
	NS 13:	¹/₈yd (15cm)

PACHRANGI STRIPE
	PS 13:	¹/₈yd (15cm)

ROWAN STRIPE
	RS 01:	¹/₄yd (23cm)
	RS 04:	¹/₈yd (15cm))
	RS 05:	¹/₄yd (23cm)

ROMAN GLASS
Gold	GP01-G:	¹/₈yd (15cm)

DAMASK
Jewel	GP02-J:	¹/₈yd (15cm)

FORGET-ME-NOT-ROSE
Jewel	GP08-J:	1¹/₄yds (1.15m)

DOTTY
Cobalt	GP14-C:	¹/₄yd (23cm)
Plum	GP14-P:	¹/₈yd (15cm)

BUBBLES
Plum	GP15-P:	¹/₄yd (23cm)

PEONY
Maroon	GP17-MR:	¹/₈yd (15cm)

AUGUST ROSES
Purple	GP18-PU:	2 yds (1.8m)

FRUIT BASKET
Gold	GP19-GD:	¹/₄yd (23cm)
Red	GP19-RD:	¹/₄yd (23cm)
Taupe	GP19-TA:	¹/₄yd (23cm)
Teal	GP19-TE:	¹/₈yd (15cm)

Quilt Assembly

= SC 02   = PS 13   = GP08-J   = GP18-PU

= SC 12   = RS 01   = GP14-C   = GP19-GD

= SC 14   = RS 04   = GP14-P   = GP19-RD

= SC 15   = RS 05   = GP15-P   = GP19-TA

= SC 31   = GP01-G   = GP17-MR   = GP19-TE

= NS 13   = GP02-J

67

Backing Fabric:
DOTTY
Plum   GP14-P: 4¹/₂yds (4.1m)
Binding Fabric:
BROAD STRIPE
              BS 08: ¹/₂yd (45cm)
Batting:
78in x 78in (198cm x 198cm).
Quilting thread:
Toning machine quilting thread.

Templates:
see page 94, 100

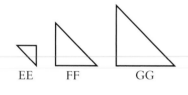

EE   FF   GG

Large square cut
9¹/₂ in x 9¹/₂ in
(24cm x 24cm)

PATCH SHAPES
The quilt centre is made up from blocks pieced from a small triangle shape (template EE). These are interspaced with large squares cut to 9¹/₂in (24cm). The blocks and squares are set 'on point' with large triangles to fill in along the quilt edges, You'll find half template GG on page xx. Take a large piece of paper, fold, place edge of template GG to fold of paper, trace around shape and cut out. Open out for the complete template. The corners are filled with a third triangle shape (template FF). The quilt also has simple borders.

CUTTING OUT
Template EE: Cut 3 ⁷/₈in- (9.75cm-) wide strips across the width of the fabric. Each strip will give you 20 patches per 45in- (114cm-) wide fabric.
Cut 36 in RS 01, GP14-C, 27 in SC 12, RS 05, GP15-P, GP19-GD, GP19-RD, GP19-TA, 18 in SC 02, SC 14, SC 15, SC 31, NS 13, PS 13, RS 04, GP01-G, GP02-J, GP14-P, GP17-MR and GP19-TE.

Template GG: Cut 2 x 14in- (35.5cm-) wide strips across the width of the fabric. Cut 4 x 14in (35.5cm) squares in GP18-PU. Using the template as a guide cut each square in half diagonally and without moving the pieces cut again across the opposite diagonal to make 4 triangles. Reserve leftover fabric for template FF.
Template FF: Cut 2 x 7¹/₄in (18.5cm) squares in GP18-PU. Cut each square in half diagonally to make 2 triangles.
Large Squares: Cut 9¹/₂in- (24cm-) wide strips across the width of the fabric. Each strip will give you 4 patches per 45in- (114cm-) wide fabric. Cut 16 x 9¹/₂in (24cm) squares in GP18-PU.
Borders: Cut 7 strips 5¹/₂in- (14cm-) wide x width of fabric in GP08-J.
Backing: Cut 1 piece 78in x 45in (198cm by 114cm), 1 piece 78in x 33¹/₂ in (193cm by 85cm) in GP14-P.
Binding: Cut 8 strips 2in- (5cm-) wide x width of fabric in BS 08.

MAKING THE QUILT CENTRE
Using a ¹/₄ in (6mm) seam allowance throughout, make up 25 blocks, use the quilt and block assembly diagrams as a guide. Arrange the blocks with the large squares and triangles (template GG) into 9 diagonal rows following the quilt assembly diagram. Join the blocks into rows, then join the rows together to form the quilt centre. Join one smaller triangle (template FF) to each corner to complete the quilt centre.

MAKING THE BORDERS
Join the 7 strips into one long length. From this cut 2 border strips to fit the quilt top and bottom. Join these to the quilt centre as indicated in the quilt assembly diagram. Then cut 2 border strips to fit the quilt sides and join to the quilt centre as indicated in the quilt assembly diagram

FINISHING THE QUILT
Press the quilt top. Seam the backing pieces using a ¹/₄in (6mm) seam allowance to form a piece approx. 78in x 78in (198cm x 198cm). Layer the quilt top, batting and backing and baste together (see page 106). Using a toning thread, in the borders and GP18-PU areas quilt a meandering pattern loosely following the floral shapes. In the pieced blocks quilt a stipple pattern on one colour only as shown in the quilting diagram. Trim the quilt edges and attach the binding (see page 107).

Block Assembly

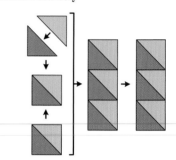

Quilting Diagram for Pieced Blocks

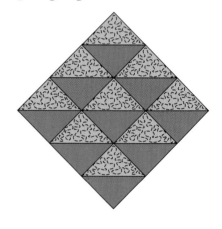

Handkerchief Corner Quilt – Pastel

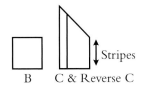

KAFFE FASSETT

N eutral elements in the quilt save it from becoming over sweet.

SIZE OF QUILT
The finished quilt will measure approx.
56in x 48in (142cm x 122cm).

MATERIALS
Patchwork Fabrics:
BLUE AND WHITE STRIPE
        BWS01: $^5/8$yd (60cm)
        BWS02: $^5/8$yd (60cm)
OMBRE STRIPE
        OS 01: $^5/8$yd (60cm)
        OS 02: $^5/8$yd (60cm)
        OS 05: $^5/8$yd (60cm)
ROMAN GLASS
Pastel   GP01-P: $^5/8$yd (60cm)
GAZANIA
Pastel   GP03-P: $^1/4$yd (23cm)

Stone   GP03-S: $^1/4$yd (23cm)
FORGET-ME-NOT ROSES
Circus   GP08-C: $^1/4$yd (23cm)
CHRYSANTHEMUM
Grey   GP13-GR: $^1/4$yd (23cm) or
           use excess from backing.
DOTTY
Terracotta GP14-T: $^2/3$yd (60cm)
BUBBLES
Grey   GP15-G: $^1/4$yd (23cm)
PEONY
Grey   GP17-GR: $^1/4$yd (23cm)
Taupe   GP17-TA: $^1/4$yd (23cm)
Violet   GP17-VI: $^1/4$yd (23cm)
FRUIT BASKET
Blue   GP19-BL: $^1/4$yd (23cm)
Pink   GP19-PK: $^1/4$yd (23cm)

Border Fabrics:
AUGUST ROSES
Pastel   GP18-PT: $^2/3$yd (60cm)
Backing Fabric:
CHRYSANTHEMUM
Grey   GP13-GR: $2^1/4$yd (2.1m)
Binding Fabric:
DOTTY
Terracotta   GP14-T: see patchwork
                fabrics
Batting:
60in x 52in (153cm x 132cm).
Quilting thread:
Toning machine quilting thread.

Templates:
see page 95, 99

B   C & Reverse C   Stripes

PATCH SHAPES
The quilt centre is made up of one square patch shape and one trapezium patch shape for the left side of each block which is reversed for the top of each block. Note: The trapezium template is provided for checking only, see instructions below for details.

CUTTING OUT
Template B: Cut $4^1/2$in- (11.5cm-) wide strips across the width of the fabric. Each strip will give you 9 patches per 45in- (114cm-) wide fabric.
Cut 7 in GP08-C, 6 in GP13-GR, 5 in GP03-P, 4 in GP03-S, 3 in GP17-TA, 2 in GP19-PK and 1 in GP19-BL, GP17-GR and GP17-VI.
Template C and Reverse C: To ensure the stripes are in the correct orientation, cut 18in- (46cm-) wide strips across the width of the fabric then cut $3^1/2$in- (9cm-) wide strips down the length of the fabric, 7 in OS 05, BWS01, 6 in OS 01, OS 02, 4 in BWS02.
Cut $1^1/2$in- (3.75cm-) wide strips across the width of the fabric. Cut 18in x $1^1/2$in (46cm x 3.75cm) strips, each strip will give you 2 patches per 45in- (114cm-) wide fabric.
Cut 11 in GP01-P, GP14-T, 8 in GP15-G.

Quilt Assembly

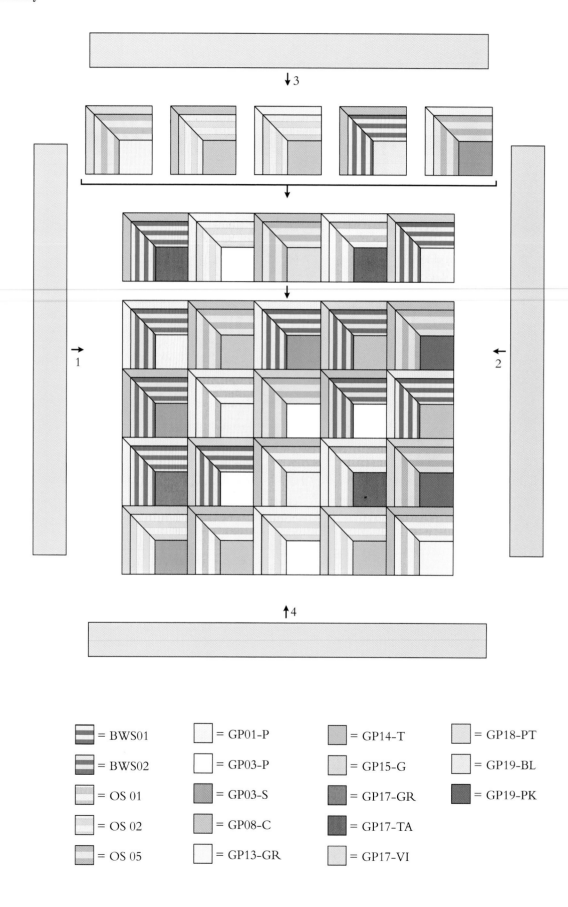

= BWS01	= GP01-P	= GP14-T	= GP18-PT
= BWS02	= GP03-P	= GP15-G	= GP19-BL
= OS 01	= GP03-S	= GP17-GR	= GP19-PK
= OS 02	= GP08-C	= GP17-TA	
= OS 05	= GP13-GR	= GP17-VI	

Borders: Cut 5 strips 4$\frac{1}{2}$in- (11.5cm-) wide across the width of the fabric in GP18-PT.

Binding: Cut 6 strips 2in- (5cm-) wide x width of fabric in GP14-T.

Backing: Cut 1 piece 60in x 45in (152cm by 114cm), 1 piece 10in x 45in (25cm by 114cm) and 1 piece 10in x 15$\frac{1}{2}$in (25cm by 39cm).

MAKING THE BLOCKS

Using a $\frac{1}{4}$in (6mm) seam allowance throughout, using the quilt assembly diagram as a guide to fabric combinations, stitch sets of 1$\frac{1}{2}$in by 18in (3.75cm by 45.5cm) and 3$\frac{1}{2}$in by 18in (9cm by 45.5cm) strips together as shown in block diagram a. Fold the joined strips in half lengthways. Matching the seam and press carefully to set the fabrics in place. Mark a 45 degree line as shown in diagram b. Stitch on the line, stopping $\frac{1}{4}$ in from the inside edge and open out the block, see diagram c. Using the guide template C and reverse C, check the size of the block by matching the diagonal line, trim the patches as necessary. Using the inset seam technique (see page 104), add the 4$\frac{1}{2}$in square (template B), see diagram d. Complete 30 blocks.

MAKING UP THE ROWS

Assemble 6 rows of 5 blocks, use the quilt assembly diagram as a guide.

MAKING THE BORDERS

Join the 5 strips to make 1 long strip. From this cut 4 borders each 48$\frac{1}{2}$in by 4$\frac{1}{2}$in (123cm x 11.5cm).

Add the borders to the quilt centre in the order indicated by the quilt assembly diagram.

FINISHING THE QUILT

Press the quilt top. Seam the backing pieces using a $\frac{1}{4}$in (6mm) seam allowance to form a piece approx. 60in x 51in (152cm by 129cm). Layer the quilt top, batting and backing and baste together (see page 106). Using a toning thread, stitch-in-the-ditch along the seam lines, between the blocks and along each border.

Trim the quilt edges and attach the binding (see page 107).

Block Assembly

a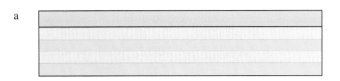

b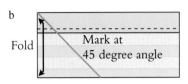

Fold

Mark at 45 degree angle

c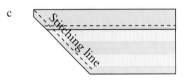

Stitching line

d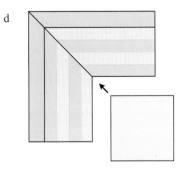

Handkerchief Corner Quilt – Dark

KAFFE FASSETT

DAMASK		
Jewel	GP02-J:	$5/8$yd (60cm)
FLORAL DANCE		
Blue	GP12-B:	$5/8$yd (60cm)
Magenta	GP12-MG:	$1/2$yd (45cm)
Ochre	GP12-O:	$5/8$yd (60cm)
CHRYSANTHEMUM		
Blue	GP13-B:	$1/2$yd (45cm)
Red	GP13-R:	$1/2$yd (45cm)
DOTTY		
Cobalt	GP14-C:	$1/4$yd (23cm)
Plum	GP14-P:	$1/4$yd (23cm)
BUBBLES		
Cobalt	GP15-C:	$1/4$yd (23cm)
Plum	GP15-P:	$1/4$yd (23cm)
PEONY		
Green	GP17-GN:	$1/4$yd (23cm)
Maroon	GP17-MR:	$1/4$yd (23cm)

Backing Fabric:
NARROW STRIPE

NS 17: 4 $3/8$yds (4m)

Bias binding Fabric:
NARROW STRIPE

NS 17: see backing fabric

Batting:
76in x 76in (193cm x 193cm).

Quilting thread:
Toning machine quilting thread.

Templates:
see page 95, 99

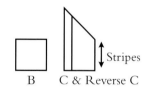

B   C & Reverse C   Stripes

PATCH SHAPES
The quilt centre is made up one square patch shape and one trapezium patch shape for the left side of each block which is reversed for the top of each block.
Note: The trapezium template is provided for checking only, see instructions below for details.

CUTTING OUT
Template B: Cut $4^1/2$in- (11.5cm-) wide strips across the width of the fabric.
Each strip will give you 9 patches per 45in- (114cm-) wide fabric.
Cut 21 in GP12-MG, 16 in GP12-B, 14 in GP12-O, 11 in GP13-R, 10 in GP02-J and 9 in GP13-B.

Flowery bandanas with bold borders were Kaffe's inspiration. The squares are 'fussy cut' to make the most of the floral fabrics

SIZE OF QUILT
The finished quilt will measure approx. 72in x 72in (183cm x 183cm).

MATERIALS
Patchwork Fabrics:
ALTERNATE STRIPE

AS 10: $5/8$yd (60cm)

BROAD CHECK

BC 03: $5/8$yd (60cm)
BC 04: $1/3$yd (30cm)

BROAD STRIPE

BS 11: $5/8$yd (60cm)

EXOTIC STRIPE

ES 10: $5/8$yd (60cm)

NARROW CHECK

NC 01: $1/3$yd (30cm)

NARROW STRIPE

NS 01: $5/8$yd (60cm)
NS 13: 1 $1/8$yd (1m)
NS 17: $5/8$yd (60cm)

PACHRANGI STRIPE

PS 08: $5/8$yd (60cm)

ROMAN GLASS

Blue & White	GP01-BW:	$1/4$yd (23cm)
Circus	GP01-C:	$5/8$yd (60cm)
Gold	GP01-G:	$1/4$yd (23cm)
Leafy	GP01-L:	$1/4$yd (23cm)
Red	GP01-R:	$1/4$yd (23cm)

Quilt Assembly

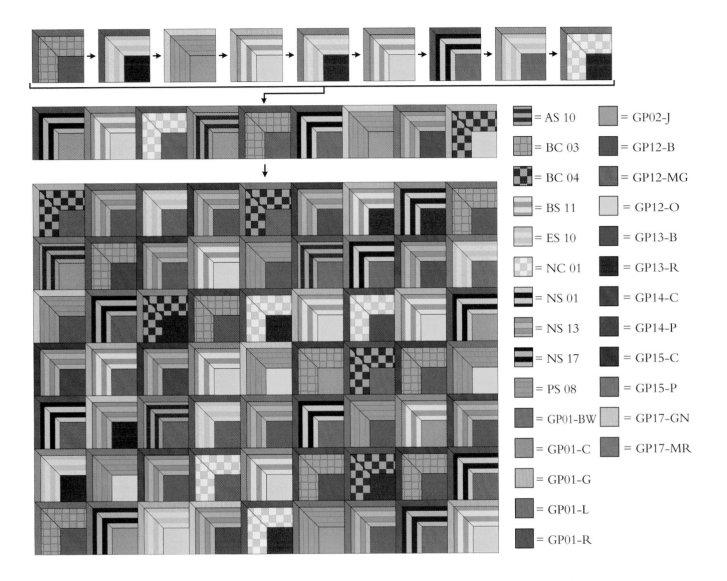

= AS 10	= GP02-J
= BC 03	= GP12-B
= BC 04	= GP12-MG
= BS 11	= GP12-O
= ES 10	= GP13-B
= NC 01	= GP13-R
= NS 01	= GP14-C
= NS 13	= GP14-P
= NS 17	= GP15-C
= PS 08	= GP15-P
= GP01-BW	= GP17-GN
= GP01-C	= GP17-MR
= GP01-G	
= GP01-L	
= GP01-R	

Template C and Reverse C: For striped fabrics, to ensure the stripes are in the correct orientation, cut 18in- (46cm-) wide strips across the width of the fabric then cut 3½in- (9cm-) wide strips down the length of the fabric. Cut 14 in NS 13, 12 in BS 11, 9 in PS 08, 8 in ES 10, NS 01, 4 in AS 10 and NS 17.

For checked fabrics, cut 3½in- (9cm-) wide strips across the width of the fabric. Cut 18in x 3½in (46cm x 9cm) strips, each strip will give you 2 patches per 45in- (114cm-) wide fabric. Cut 10 in BC 03, 6 in BC 04 and NC 01.

Cut 1½in- (3.75cm-) wide strips across the width of the fabric. Cut 18in x 1½in (46cm x 3.75cm) strips, each strip will give you 2 patches per 45in- (114cm-) wide fabric.

Cut 11 in GP01-C, 10 in GP14-P, GP01-R, 9 in GP01-G, 8 in GP15-C, GP17-MR, 6 in GP14-C, GP17-GN, 5 in GP01-L, GP15-P, 3 in GP01-BW.

Backing: Cut 1 piece 76in x 45in (193cm by 114cm), 1 piece 76in x 31½ in (193cm by 80cm) in NS 17, reserve the leftover piece for binding.

Bias binding: Cut 8½ yds (7.75m) of 2½in- (6.5cm-) wide bias binding from NS 17.

MAKING THE BLOCKS

See this section in the Handkerchief Corners Quilt - Pastel on page71.

MAKING UP THE ROWS

Assemble 9 rows of 9 blocks, use the quilt assembly diagram as a guide.

FINISHING THE QUILT

Press the quilt top.

Seam the backing pieces using a ¼in (6mm) seam allowance to form a piece approx. 76in x 76in (193cm by 193cm). Layer the quilt top, batting and backing and baste together (see page 106). Using a toning thread, stitch-in-the-ditch along the seam lines between the blocks. You could also outline the floral motifs with free machine quilting if you wish. Trim the quilt edges and attach the binding (see page 107).

Jubilee Garden Quilt

KAFFE FASSETT

With colours like a stained glass lamp this quilt would be delightful in an orangerie thrown over a huge sofa or hammock.

SIZE OF QUILT

The finished quilt will measure approx. 128^1/2in x 93^1/2in (326cm x 238cm).

MATERIALS

Patchwork Fabrics:

BROAD CHECK

| | BC 01: 1yd (90cm) |

OMBRE STRIPE

| | OS 05: ^{3}/4yd (70cm) |

ROWAN STRIPE

| | RS 06: 1^1/4yd (1.15m) |

ROMAN GLASS
Gold   GP01-G: ^{1}/4yd (23cm)
Leafy   GP01-L: 1^1/4yd (1.15m)

DAMASK
Jewel   GP02-J: ^{5}/8yd (60cm)
Pastel   GP02-P: ^{3}/4yd (70cm)

GAZANIA
Pastel   GP03-P: ^{1}/8yd (15cm)

ARTICHOKES
Leafy   GP07-L: ^{3}/8yd (35cm)
Pastel   GP07-P: ^{1}/2yd (45cm)

Jewel   GP08-J: 1 yd (90cm)

FLORAL DANCE
Magenta   GP12-MG: ^{3}/8yd (35cm)
Ochre   GP12-O: 1^1/4yd (1.15m)
Pink   GP12-P: 1^1/4yd (1.15m)

CHRYSANTHEMUM
Green   GP13-GN: 1^3/4yds (1.6m)
Ochre   GP13-O: ^{1}/2yd (45cm)

DOTTY
Lavender   GP14-L: 1 yd (90cm)
Ochre   GP14-O: ^{3}/4yd (70cm)
Terracotta GP14-T: ^{1}/8yd (15cm)

BUBBLES
Grey   GP15-G: ^{1}/8yd (15cm)
Ochre   GP15-O: ^{1}/4yd (23cm)

Backing Fabric:
CHRYSANTHEMUM
Green   GP13-GN: 8^1/2yds (3.1m)

Binding Fabric:
CHRYSANTHEMUM
Green   GP13-GN: ^{3}/4yd (70cm)

Batting:
133in x 98in (338cm x 249cm).
Quilting thread:
Toning hand or machine quilting thread.

Templates:
see page 94, 95, 97

PATCH SHAPES

The quilt made up of one diamond patch shape (Template Z) and three triangle patch shapes (X & reverse X, Y and AA) which are used to fill in around the edges of the quilt.

CUTTING OUT

Template Y: To ensure the stripe direction is in the correct orientation for fabric RS 06 cut 1 x 16in- (40.5cm-) wide strip across the width of the fabric. From this piece cut 14 x 2^1/4in- (5.75cm-) wide strips down the length of the fabric, each strip will give you 3 patches of template Y. Cut 40 in RS 06. Reserve the remaining fabric for Templates X & reverse X.

Template X and Reverse X: From the remaining RS 06 fabric Cut 1 x 2^1/2in- (6.5cm-) wide strip down the length of the fabric. Cut 2 in RS 06, reverse the template and cut 2 more in RS 06.

Template Z: To ensure the stripe direction is in the correct orientation for fabric OS 05 cut 1 x 18in- (46cm-) wide strip across the width of the fabric. Cut 40 in OS 05.

To ensure the stripe direction is in the correct orientation for fabric RS 06 cut 1 x 19in- (48.5cm-) wide strip across the width of the fabric. Cut 42 in RS 06.

For all other fabrics, cut 3^1/2in- (9cm-) wide strips across the width of the fabric. Each strip will give you 10 patches per 45in- (114cm-) wide fabric. Cut 162 in GP13-GN, 108 in GP12-P, 104 in GP12-O, 92 in GP01-L, 80 in GP14-O, 76 in GP08-J, 68 in GP02-P, 64 in GP14-O, 42 in GP02-J, 40 in BC 01, GP13-O, 36 in GP07-P, 28 in GP07-L, 24 in GP12-MG, 16 in GP01-G, 12 in GP15-O, 8 in GP03-P, 4 in GP14-T and 1 in GP15-G.

Template AA: Cut 3^3/4in- (9.5cm-) wide strips across the width of the fabric. Each strip will give you 19 patches per 45in- (114cm-) wide fabric. Cut 44 in BC 01, 4 in GP01-L and OS 05.

Quilt Assembly

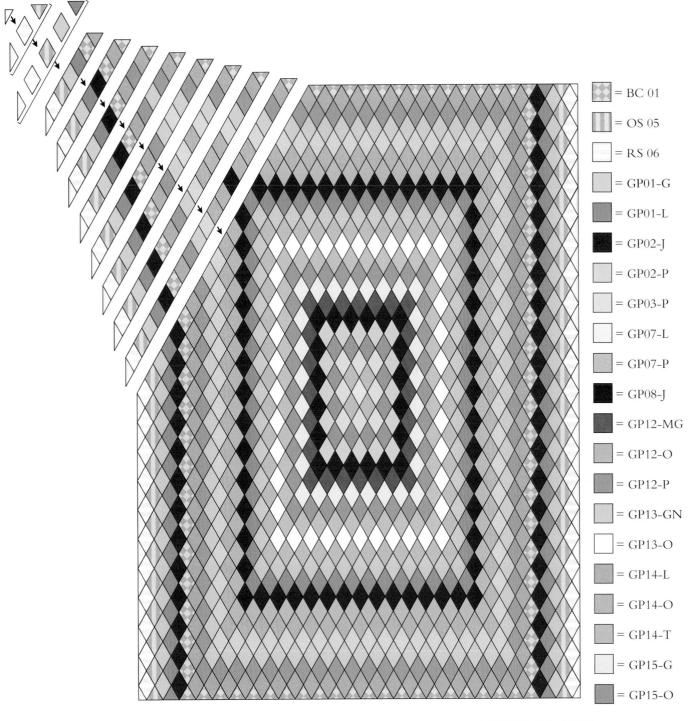

= BC 01

= OS 05

= RS 06

= GP01-G

= GP01-L

= GP02-J

= GP02-P

= GP03-P

= GP07-L

= GP07-P

= GP08-J

= GP12-MG

= GP12-O

= GP12-P

= GP13-GN

= GP13-O

= GP14-L

= GP14-O

= GP14-T

= GP15-G

= GP15-O

Binding: cut 11 strips 2in- (5cm-) wide x width of fabric in GP13-GN.

Backing: Cut 3 pieces 98in x 45in (249cm by 114cm) in GP13-GN.

MAKING THE QUILT

Using a ¹/4in (6mm) seam allowance throughout, join the diamond patches (template Z) into rows, filling in along the top edge of the quilt with template AA, the sides of the quilt with template Y and the extreme corners with templates X & reverse X, as shown in the quilt assembly diagram.

Refer to the quilt assembly diagram for fabric sequence, laying each row out in turn will help to keep the fabric sequence correct.

FINISHING THE QUILT

Press the quilt top. Seam the backing pieces using a ¹/4in (6mm) seam allowance to form a piece approx. 133in x 98in (338cm x 249cm). Layer the quilt top, batting and backing and baste together (see page 106). Using a toning thread, stitch-in-the-ditch along the seam lines, between the patches by hand or machine. Trim the quilt edges and attach the binding (see page 107).

Orange Grove Quilt

SANDY DONABED

This is an improvisational quilt and these are more guidelines than directions. The way to start is by finding a multi-coloured fabric you love and to key all the other choices from that. In this case the choice was one of Kaffe's stripes, Pachrangi stripe 13 (PS 13). From your choice you can then pull out about 15 other fabrics in colours that work. For this quilt the colours were all the greens and oranges available in the shot cotton range that are reminiscent of the orange groves lining the roadsides in Florida.

SIZE OF QUILT
The finished quilt will measure approx. 54$\frac{1}{2}$in x 42$\frac{1}{2}$in (138cm x 108cm).

MATERIALS
Patchwork Fabrics:
SHOT COTTON
Ginger   SC 01: $\frac{1}{2}$yd (45cm)

Cassis	SC 02: $\frac{1}{2}$yd (45cm)	
Bittersweet	SC 10: $\frac{1}{2}$yd (45cm)	
Tangerine	SC 11: $\frac{1}{2}$yd (45cm)	
Chartreuse	SC 12: see border fabrics	
Mustard	SC 16: $\frac{1}{2}$yd (45cm)	
Sage	SC 17: $\frac{1}{2}$yd (45cm)	
Tobacco	SC 18: $\frac{1}{2}$yd (45cm)	
Lichen	SC 19: $\frac{1}{2}$yd (45cm)	
Pine	SC 21: $\frac{1}{2}$yd (45cm)	
Pewter	SC 22: $\frac{1}{2}$yd (45cm)	
Stone Grey	SC 23: $\frac{1}{2}$yd (45cm)	
Ecru	SC 24: $\frac{1}{2}$yd (45cm)	
Duck Egg	SC 26: $\frac{1}{2}$yd (45cm)	
Grass	SC 27: $\frac{1}{2}$yd (45cm)	
Lemon	SC 34: $\frac{1}{2}$yd (45cm)	
Sunshine	SC 35: $\frac{1}{2}$yd (45cm)	
Apple	SC 39: $\frac{1}{2}$yd (45cm)	
Rush	SC 42: $\frac{1}{2}$yd (45cm)	
Lime	SC 43: $\frac{1}{2}$yd (45cm)	

Note: these quantities are the maximum you will need. Buy the full $\frac{1}{2}$yd (45cm) of the colours you like especially and less of others. In total you will need about 4yds (3.7m) of shot cottons plus the leftovers from the borders.

PACHRANGI STRIPE
     PS 13: 1yd (90cm)
Sandy also used a selection of other stripes from the Kaffe Fassett fabric range in small quantities.

Border Fabrics:
SHOT COTTON
Chartreuse   SC 12: 1yd (90cm) use excess in patchwork.

Backing Fabric:
PACHRANGI STRIPE
     PS 13: 2 $\frac{5}{8}$yds (2.4m)

Binding Fabric:
PACHRANGI STRIPE
     PS 13: $\frac{1}{2}$yd (45cm) or use leftover from backing fabric

Batting:
58in x 46in (148cm x 117cm).

Quilting thread:
Variegated machine quilting thread.

Template:
see page 97

W

PATCH SHAPES
The quilt is made using 'composite fabric' (see page 79) constructed from strips cut from multiple fabrics. Triangles (template W) are then cut from the composite fabric. The remaining fabric is cut into 2in - (5cm-) wide sashing strips. The triangles and strips are then made into blocks.

Quilt Assembly

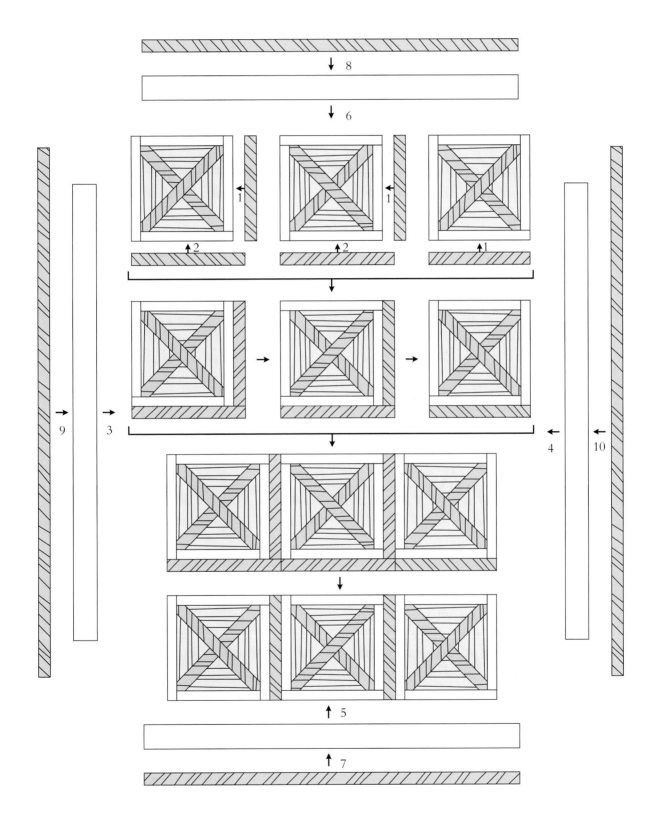

Block Assembly

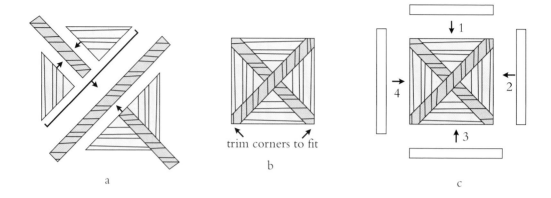

a

b

trim corners to fit

c

Cutting Diagram for Triangles and Sashing

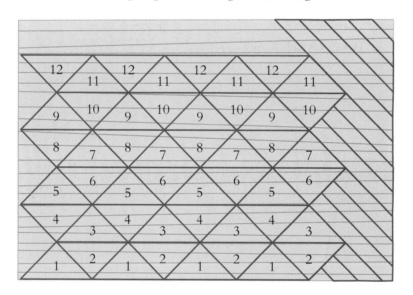

CUTTING OUT

Borders: Cut 5 strips 3in- (7.5cm-) wide x width of the fabric in SC 12. Use the remaining fabric for strips as described below.

Strips to Make Composite Fabric: Cut strips approximately 1-2in (2.5-5cm) wide across the width of the fabric in all the shot cottons and PS 13 plus any other striped fabrics you have decided to add. The strips do not need to be regular, they can be narrow at one end and wider at the other. **Note:** Sandy says, 'remember this is supposed to be improvisational and liberating! Don't measure for this, instead just free-cut the strips, you can even piece the strips if you want to add additional colours here and there'.

Backing: Cut 1 piece 46in x 45in (117cm x 114cm) and 1 piece 46in x 14$\frac{1}{2}$in (117cm x 37cm) in PS 13.

Binding: Cut 5 strips 2in- (5cm-) wide x width of fabric in PS 13

MAKING THE COMPOSITE FABRIC

Using a $\frac{1}{4}$in (6mm) seam allowance throughout, stitch strips of fabric together, varying the colour combinations to make 2 pieces of composite fabric at least 30in (76cm) long by the width of the strips, about 45in (114cm). Press the seams carefully from the back in one direction. Steam press the fabric again from the front so it lays very flat. Trim the edges of the composite fabric to square it up. Set aside any unused strips of shot cotton fabric.

CUTTING THE SASHING AND TRIANGLES

Take one piece of composite fabric and cut the entire piece into 2in (5cm) wide 45 degree diagonal strips.
Note: Be careful not to pull these strips since they are all on the bias and will distort easily.
On the second piece of composite fabric, draw a grid of triangles (Using template W) on the diagonal to the stripe direction as shown in the cutting diagram for triangles and sashing. Cut the triangles and keep them in 12 sets of 4 triangles as

indicated by the numbers on the diagram. Note: If you make a larger piece of fabric to start, you can increase the size or number of the triangles and thus the size of the quilt. The remainder of the fabric can then be cut into 2in (5cm) diagonal strips for use as sashing.

MAKING THE BLOCKS

In turn take each set of triangles, two short and one longer length of sashing. Join the sashing to the triangles as shown in diagram a, press the seams towards the triangles. Trim the sashing to fit as shown in diagram b. You will end up with blocks approximately 9in (22.75cm) square.

Note: For this quilt the 4 triangles in each block are the same, but you might want to consider mixing them up even further before sewing them together. Add the reserved shot cotton strips to each edge of each block as shown in diagram c trimming to fit as you go, again trying to not pay attention to colour arrangement. Press, and trim the 12 blocks to 11in (28cm) square.

MAKING THE ROWS

Assemble the blocks into 4 rows of 3 blocks, adding sashing to the rows as indicated in the quilt assembly diagram. Join the rows to form the quilt centre.

ADDING THE BORDERS

Join the 5 border strips to form one long length, from this cut 2 borders to fit the quilt sides and join to the quilt centre.
Then cut 2 borders to fit the quilt top and bottom and join to the quilt centre.
The outer border is made using more of the 2in- (5cm-) wide sashing strips. Join enough into 2 lengths to fit the quilt top and bottom and join to the quilt centre. Repeat for the quilt sides.

FINISHING THE QUILT

Press the quilt top. Layer the quilt top, batting and backing and baste together (see page 106).
Using a toning machine quilting thread, stitch a chevron pattern about 2in (5cm) apart across the surface of the quilt. Trim the quilt edges and attach the binding (see page 107).

Pete's Paul Quilt

ROBERTA HORTON

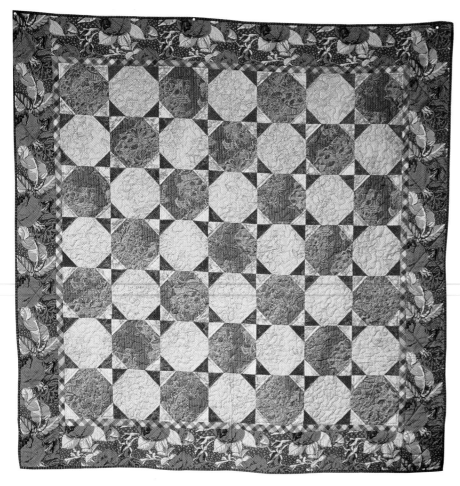

R oberta used the traditional Robbing Peter to Pay Paul block to showcase the old fashioned two-tone toiles. The brightly coloured large floral border provides a dramatic contrast.

SIZE OF QUILT

The finished quilt will measure approx. 67^1/2in x 67^1/2in (171.5cm x 171.5cm).

MATERIALS

Patchwork Fabrics:
BROAD CHECK
　　　　　　BC 01: ^{1}/2yd (45cm)
AUGUST ROSES
Magenta　　GP18-MG: 2 yds (1.80m)
FRUIT BASKET
Apricot　　GP19-AP: ^{7}/8yd (80cm)
Red　　　　GP19-RD: ^{7}/8yd (80cm)
Taupe　　　GP19-TA: 1^1/4yd (1.15m)
Teal　　　　GP19-TE: 1^1/4yd (1.15m)

Backing Fabric:
PACHRANGI STRIPE
　　　　　　PS 01: 4yds (3.7m)

Binding Fabric:
PACHRANGI STRIPE
　　　　　　PS 01: see backing fabric

Batting:
71in x 71in (181cm x 181cm).

Quilting thread:
Grey and Russet Red machine quilting thread.

Template:
see page 96

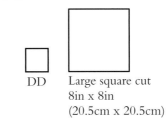

DD　　Large square cut
8in x 8in
(20.5cm x 20.5cm)

PATCH SHAPES

The quilt centre is made using a traditional Robbing Peter to Pay Paul block, made from an octagon and four triangles. This block is made 'the easy way' by using two sizes of squares. A template is provided for the smaller square (template DD), the larger is cut to 8in (20.5cm).

CUTTING OUT

Template DD: Cut 3in- (7.5cm-) wide strips across the width of the fabric. Each strip will give you 14 patches per 45in- (114cm-) wide fabric.
Cut 100 in GP19-AP and 96 in GP19-RD.
Large Squares: Cut 8in- (20.5cm-) wide strips across the width of the fabric. Each strip will give you 5 patches per 45in- (114cm-) wide fabric.
Cut 25 in GP19-TE and 24 in GP19-TA.
Inner borders: Cut 4^3/4yds of 1^1/2in- (3.75cm-) wide bias strips from BC 01.
Outer borders: Cut from the length of the fabric, 2 strips 6^1/2in x 55in (16.5cm x 139.75cm) and 2 strips 6^1/2in x 67in (16.5cm x 170cm).
Backing: Cut 1 piece 71in x 45in (181cm x 114cm) and 1 piece 71in x 26^1/2in (181cm x 67.5cm) in PS 01, reserve the leftover piece for the binding.
Binding: Cut 4 strips 2in- (5cm-) wide x length of fabric in PS 01.

MAKING THE QUILT

Using a ^{1}/4in (6mm) seam allowance throughout, make a total of 49 Robbing Peter to Pay Paul blocks. See the instructions for this block in the Beyond the Pale Quilt on page 46. Follow the quilt assembly diagram for fabric placement.

MAKING UP THE ROWS

Assemble 7 rows of 7 blocks, use the quilt assembly diagram as a guide. Make sure to maintain the dark/light checkerboard alternating of the blocks.

MAKING THE BORDERS

Join the 1^1/2in (3.75cm) into 2 strips 53in (138.5cm) and 2 strips 55in (139.75cm). Handle the bias strips carefully as they will be stretchy. Add the inner borders to the quilt centre in the order indicated in the quilt assembly diagram. Repeat in the same way for the outer borders.

Quilt Assembly

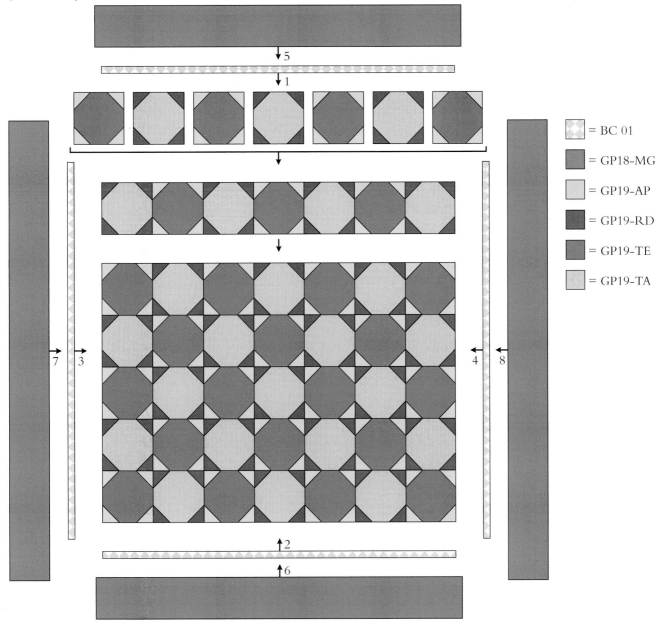

= BC 01

= GP18-MG

= GP19-AP

= GP19-RD

= GP19-TE

= GP19-TA

FINISHING THE QUILT

Press the quilt top. Seam the backing pieces using a $^1/4$in (6mm) seam allowance to form a piece approx. 71in x 71in (181cm x 181cm).

Layer the quilt top, batting and backing and baste together (see page 106).

Using a grey machine quilting thread, machine stitch-in-the-ditch along the seam lines of the rows, and the inner and outer borders both horizontally and vertically.

Using russet red machine quilting thread, echo quilt where the small triangles come together to form a diamond at the block intersections.

Meander quilt in the octagonal areas. Quilt the borders using russet red machine quilting thread as shown in the quilting diagram being careful to leave a $^1/4$in (6mm) seam allowance free of quilting so that the binding will not obscure the pattern. Trim the quilt edges and attach the binding (see page 107).

Quilting Diagram

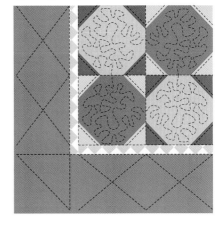

Strippy Chevrons Quilt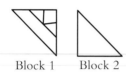

SUSAN DRUDING

Backing Fabric:
BROAD STRIPE

BS 06: 2yds (1.85m)

Binding Fabric:
BROAD STRIPE

BS 06: see backing fabric

Batting:
49in x 49in (125cm x 125cm).
Quilting thread:
Toning machine quilting thread.

Foundation Blocks:
see page 99

Block 1   Block 2

FOUNDATION PAPERS

The quilt centre is made up of two triangular free-hand foundation blocks. The blocks are pieced in pairs to make squares. You will find examples of the foundation blocks, printed at 50% size at the back of this book to use as a stitching guide (see page 99).

CUTTING OUT

Important Note: The only colours shown accurately in the diagram are the corner squares and triangles for Block 1. The colours shown on the striped sections give a general indication of colour distribution.

Block 1: In preparation for foundation piecing pre-cut freehand a total of 37 approximately 3in- (7.5cm-) squares (they do not need to be perfectly square) from the following fabrics: GP01-C, GP01-J, GP01-L, GP01-P, GP01-R, GP15-C, GP15-P, GP15-S. Cut a total of 37 x 4in (10cm) squares in the following fabrics: SC 05, SC 08, SC 35, SC 41, SC 42. Cut the squares in half diagonally to make 74 triangles. These quantities allow for a practice block.

Cut 1-1^1/2in- (2.5-3.75cm-) wide strips across the width of your light fabric selections. The strips do not need to be regular.

Block 2: Cut 1-1^1/2in- (2.5-3.75cm-) wide strips across the width of your dark fabric selections. The strips do not need to be regular.

T his unusual scrap style quilt uses the free-hand foundation method for piecing. If any of your blocks are a little undersized you can copy Susan's idea and use a 'rogue' strip which may span a couple of blocks.

SIZE OF QUILT
The finished quilt will measure approx. 45in x 45in (114cm x 114cm).

MATERIALS
Patchwork Fabrics for corner squares and triangles in Block 1:
SHOT COTTON
Opal	SC 05: ^{1}/8yd (15cm)
Raspberry	SC 08: ^{1}/8yd (15cm)
Sunshine	SC 35: ^{1}/8yd (15cm)
Jade	SC 41: ^{1}/8yd (15cm)
Rush	SC 42: ^{1}/8yd (15cm)

ROMAN GLASS
Circus	GP01-C: ^{1}/8yd (15cm)

Jewel	GP01-J:	^{1}/8yd (15cm)
Leafy	GP01-L:	^{1}/8yd (15cm)
Pastel	GP01-P:	^{1}/8yd (15cm)
Red	GP01-R:	^{1}/8yd (15cm)

BUBBLES
Cobalt	GP15-C:	^{1}/8yd (15cm)
Plum	GP15-P:	^{1}/8yd (15cm)
Sky Blue	GP15-S:	^{1}/8yd (15cm)

Other Patchwork Fabrics:
Block 1: A total of 1^1/2yds (1.4m) in a selection of light shot cotton, prints and stripes
Block 2: A total of 2 yds (1.85m) in a selection of dark shot cotton, prints and stripes.

Quilt Assembly

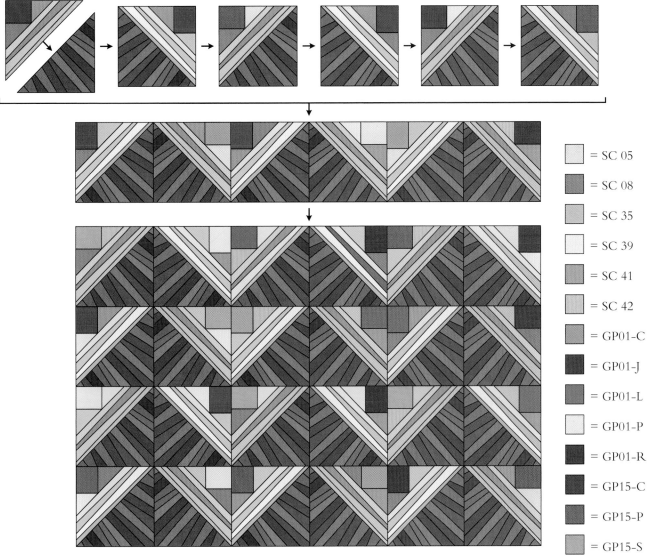

= SC 05
= SC 08
= SC 35
= SC 39
= SC 41
= SC 42
= GP01-C
= GP01-J
= GP01-L
= GP01-P
= GP01-R
= GP15-C
= GP15-P
= GP15-S

Note: The only colours shown accurately in the diagram are the corner squares and triangles for Block 1. The colours shown on the striped sections give a general indication of colour distribution.

Backing: Cut 1 piece 49in x 45in (124.5cm x 114cm), 1 piece 4^1/2 in x 45in (11.5cm x 114cm) and 1 piece 4^1/2in x 4^1/2in (11.5cm x 11.5cm) in BS 06.

Binding: Cut 5 strips 2in- (5cm-) wide x width of fabric in BS 06.

MAKING THE BLOCKS
Make up 36 of Block 1 and 36 of Block 2

using the free-hand foundation piecing method (see page 105).

MAKING UP THE ROWS
Piece pairs of Block 1 and Block 2 to make squares, press the seam allowance open to reduce bulk. Assemble the quilt into 6 rows of 6 blocks as shown in the quilt assembly diagram. Join the rows to form the quilt centre. Remove the foundation papers.

FINISHING THE QUILT
Press the quilt top. Seam the backing pieces using a ^{1}/4in (6mm) seam allowance to form a piece approx. 49in x 49in (125cm x 125cm). Layer the quilt top, batting and backing and baste together (see page 106). Using a toning thread, quilt in a giant snakelike meandering pattern across the surface of the quilt. Trim the quilt edges and attach the binding (see page107).

Mosaic Columns Quilt

KAFFE FASSETT

Backing Fabric:
GAZANIA
Pastel   GP03-P: 8 yds (7.3m)
Binding Fabric:
PEONY
Blue   GP17-BL: ^{3}/4yd (70cm)
Batting:
94in x 106in (239cm x 269cm).
Quilting thread:
Toning machine quilting thread.

Templates:
see page 99, 101

HH   II

B   Large square cut
8^1/2in x 8^1/2in
(21.5cm x 21.5cm)

A typical layout for an early chintz quilt, jazzed up by the high pastel palette and mosaic fabrics.

SIZE OF QUILT
The finished quilt will measure approx. 90^1/2in x 102in (230cm x 259cm).

MATERIALS
Patchwork Fabrics:
OMBRE STRIPE
          OS 02: ^{3}/8yd (35cm)
ROWAN STRIPE
          RS 05: ^{3}/8yd (35cm)
ROMAN GLASS
Pink   GP01-PK: ^{3}/8yd (35cm)
GAZANIA
Circus   GP03-C: ^{3}/8yd (35cm)
Pastel   GP03-P: ^{3}/8yd (35cm) or
          use leftover from backing.
ARTICHOKES
Pastel   GP07-P: ^{3}/8yd (35cm)
FORGET-ME-NOT-ROSE
Circus   GP08-C: ^{3}/8yd (35cm)
FLORAL DANCE
Ochre   GP12-O: ^{3}/8yd (35cm)
Pink   GP12-P: ^{1}/4yd (23cm)

CHRYSANTHEMUM
Ochre   GP13-O: ^{3}/8yd (35cm)
DOTTY
Driftwood   GP14-D: ^{3}/8yd (35cm)
Lavender   GP14-L: ^{3}/8yd (35cm)
BUBBLES
Grey   GP15-G: ^{3}/8yd (35cm)
Ochre   GP15-O: ^{3}/8yd (35cm)
Sky Blue   GP15-S: ^{3}/8yd (35cm)
MOSAIC
Blue   GP16-BL: ^{3}/4yd (70cm)
Pink   GP16-PK: 2 yds (1.8m)
PEONY
Blue   GP17-BL: ^{3}/8yd (35cm)
Grey   GP17-GR: ^{3}/8yd (35cm)
Ochre   GP17-OC: ^{3}/8yd (35cm)
Red   GP17-RD: ^{3}/8yd (35cm)
Violet   GP17-VI: ^{3}/8yd (35cm)
AUGUST ROSES
Pink   GP18-PK: 1^1/2yds (1.4m)
FRUIT BASKET
Apricot   GP19-AP: ^{3}/8yd (35cm)
Blue   GP19-BL: ^{3}/8yd (35cm)

PATCH SHAPES
The quilt centre is made up from small square patches (template B), pieced into four patch blocks. These are interspaced with large squares cut to 8^1/2in (21.5cm). The blocks and squares are set 'on point' with a large triangle (template II) to fill in along the quilt edges, You'll find half template II on page xx. Take a large piece of paper, fold, place edge of template II to fold of paper, trace around shape and cut out. Open out for the complete template. The corners are filled with a second triangle shape (template HH).

CUTTING OUT
Template B: Cut 4^1/2in- (11.5cm-) wide strips across the width of the fabric.
Each strip will give you 9 patches per 45in- (114cm-) wide fabric.
Cut 18 in GP03-C GP13-O, 16 in GP12-O, GP15-G, GP15-O, GP17-GR, GP17-OC, GP17-VI, 14 in RS 05, GP07-P, GP19-BL, 12 in OS 02, GP08-C, GP14-L, GP19-AP, 10 in GP01-PK, GP03-P, GP14-D, GP15-S, GP17-BL, GP17-RD and 6 in GP12-P.

Quilt Assembly

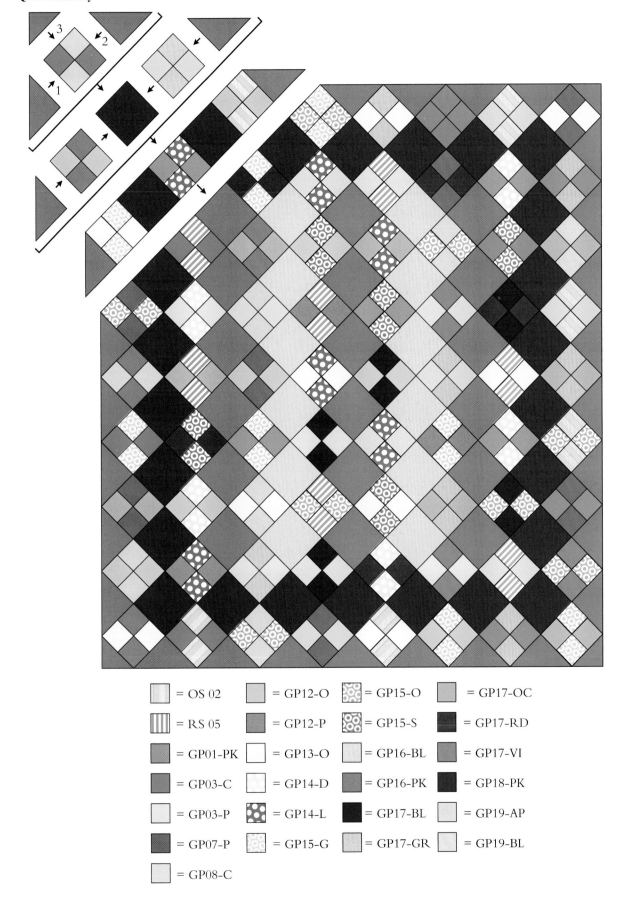

= OS 02	= GP12-O	= GP15-O	= GP17-OC
= RS 05	= GP12-P	= GP15-S	= GP17-RD
= GP01-PK	= GP13-O	= GP16-BL	= GP17-VI
= GP03-C	= GP14-D	= GP16-PK	= GP18-PK
= GP03-P	= GP14-L	= GP17-BL	= GP19-AP
= GP07-P	= GP15-G	= GP17-GR	= GP19-BL
= GP08-C			

Diagonal Squares Cushion

PAULINE SMITH

Template HH: Cut 3 x 12^1/$_2$in- (31.75cm-) wide strips across the width of the fabric. Cut 8 x 12^1/$_2$in (31.75cm) squares in GP16-PK. Using the template as a guide cut each square in half diagonally and without moving the pieces cut again across the opposite diagonal to make 4 triangles. Reserve leftover fabric for template II.

Template II: Cut 2 x 6^1/$_2$in (16.5cm) squares in GP16-PK. Cut each square in half diagonally to make 2 triangles.

Large Squares: Cut 8^1/$_2$in- (21.5cm-) wide strips across the width of the fabric. Each strip will give you 5 patches per 45in- (114cm-) wide fabric. Cut 26 x 8^1/$_2$in (21.5cm) squares in GP18-PK, 18 in GP16-PK and 12 in GP16-BL.

Backing: Cut 2 pieces 94in x 45in (239cm by 114cm), and 1 piece 94in x 13^1/$_2$ in (239cm by 34cm) in GP03-P.

Binding: Cut 10 strips 2in- (5cm-) wide x width of fabric in GP17-BL.

MAKING THE BLOCKS

Using a ^{1}/$_4$in (6mm) seam allowance throughout, make up 72 four patch blocks, use the block assembly diagram for Beyond the Pale Quilt block 1 on page 46 as a guide to piecing and the quilt assembly diagram as a guide to fabric combinations.

MAKING THE ROWS

Arrange the blocks with the large squares and triangles (template GG) into 16 diagonal rows following the quilt assembly diagram. Join the blocks into rows, then join the rows together to form the quilt centre. Join one smaller triangle (template II) to each corner to complete the quilt centre.

FINISHING THE QUILT

Press the quilt top. Seam the backing pieces using a ^{1}/$_4$in (6mm) seam allowance to form a piece approx. 94in x 106in (239cm x 269cm). Layer the quilt top, batting and backing and baste together (see page 106). Using a toning thread, quilt a meandering pattern loosely following the floral and leaf shapes, or alternatively stitch-in-the-ditch along the seam lines. Trim the quilt edges and attach the binding (see page 107).

This stylish and subtle cushion, on the right of this photograph, is a quick and easy project, ideal for a weekend.

SIZE OF CUSHION

The finished quilt will measure approx. 16in x 16in (40.5cm x 40.5cm).

MATERIALS

Patchwork Fabrics:

SHOT COTTON

Slate	SC 04:	^{1}/$_8$yd (15cm)
Raspberry	SC 08:	^{1}/$_8$yd (15cm)
Denim	SC 15:	^{1}/$_4$yd (23cm)
Charcoal	SC 25:	^{1}/$_8$yd (15cm)
Mushroom	SC 31:	^{1}/$_8$yd (15cm)
Biscuit	SC 38:	^{1}/$_3$yd (30cm)

Template:
see page 97

I

PATCH SHAPES

This cushion is made from a single square template (template I see page xx) framed with simple borders. The reverse is made in an envelope style with strips of fabric cut to size.

CUTTING OUT

Template I: Cut 2in- (5cm-) wide strips across the width of the fabric. Each strip will give you 22 patches per 45in- (114cm-) wide fabric.

Cut 15 in SC 04, 12 in SC 15 and SC 31, 11 in SC 25, 7 in SC 08 and SC 38.

Borders: Cut 2 strips 2^1/$_2$in x 12^1/$_2$in (6.5cm x 31.75cm) and 2 strips 2^1/$_2$in x 16^1/$_2$in (6.5cm x 42cm) in SC 38

Diagonal Squares Cushion Assembly

Diagonal Squares Back

↓ 4

1 ↑   2 ←

↑ 3

■ = SC 04

■ = SC 08

■ = SC 15

■ = SC 25

□ = SC 31

□ = SC 38

overlap

Cushion Reverse: Cut 1 piece 16^1/$_2$in x 10in (42cm x 25.5cm) in SC 38, 1 piece 3^3/$_4$in x 10^1/$_2$ in (9.5cm x 26.5cm) in SC 04, SC 08, SC 15, SC 25 and SC 31, 1 piece 17in x 2^1/$_4$in (43cm x 5.75cm) in SC 15.

MAKING THE CUSHION FRONT
Using a ^{1}/$_4$in (6mm) seam allowance throughout, make up the cushion centre as shown in the diagrams, then add the borders in the order shown.

MAKING THE CUSHION REVERSE
Stitch the 3^3/$_4$in x 10in (9.5cm x 25.5cm) pieces together in the order indicated in the cushion reverse diagram. Bind the edge using the 17in x 2^1/$_4$in (43cm x 5.75cm) piece in SC 15. Trim the resulting rectangle to 16^1/$_2$in x 10in (42cm x 25.5cm). Take the 16^1/$_2$in x 10in (42cm x 25.5cm) piece in SC 38, press a double ^{1}/$_2$in (1.2cm) hem to the wrong side of one long edge and stitch in place, close to the first pressed edge.

FINISHING THE CUSHION
To finish the cushions follow the instruction on page 89.

Easy Peasy Cushion 🧵

PAULINE SMITH

The central panel of this unusual cushion has 'wonky' pieces and no matching seams. The panel is trimmed to size after piecing, making it a great project for a beginner.

SIZE OF CUSHION
The finished quilt will measure approx. 16in x 16in (40.5cm x 40.5cm).

MATERIALS
Patchwork Fabrics:
SHOT COTTON

Slate	SC 04:	$1/8$yd (15cm)
Raspberry	SC 08:	$1/8$yd (15cm)
Denim	SC 15:	$1/8$yd (15cm)
Ecru	SC 24:	$1/8$yd (15cm)
Charcoal	SC 25:	$1/8$yd (23cm)
Mushroom	SC 31:	$1/8$yd (15cm)
Biscuit	SC 38:	$1/4$yd (23cm)

PATCH SHAPES
The central panel is made from 4 pieced strips of varying widths framed with simple, irregular borders. The reverse is made in an envelope style with strips of fabric cut to size.

CUTTING OUT
Central Panel:
Strip 1: Cut 1 piece $2^3/4$in x 8in (7cm x 20cm) in SC 31, 1 piece $2^3/4$in x 5in (7cm by 12.75cm) in SC 24.
Strip 2: Cut 1 piece $1^3/4$in x 5in (4.5cm x 12.75cm) in SC 31, 1 piece $1^3/4$in x 7in (4.5cm by 17.5cm) in SC 04.
Strip 3: Cut 1 piece $2^1/4$in x 8in (5.75cm x 20cm) in SC 08, 1 piece $2^1/4$in x 4in (5.75cm by 10cm) in SC 15.
Strip 4: Cut 1 piece $4^1/2$in x $7^1/2$in (11.5cm x 19cm) in SC 04, 1 piece $4^1/2$in x 5in (11.5cm by 12.75cm) in SC 38, 1 piece $1^3/4$in x $3^3/4$in (4.5cm x 9.5cm)* and 1 piece $1^3/4$in x 1in (4.5cm x 2.5cm)*.
* Sew these with short ends together before sewing into the strip.
Borders: Cut 1 piece $7^3/4$in x $4^1/4$in (19.5cm x 10.75cm) in SC 38, 1 piece $12^1/2$in x $4^1/4$in (31.75cm x 10.75cm) in SC 38, 1 piece $12^1/2$in x 3in (31.75cm x 7.5cm) in SC 25. 1 piece 14in x $4^1/2$in (35.5cm x 11.5cm) in SC 25, 1 piece $16^1/2$in x 3in (42cm x 7.5cm) in SC 04.
Cushion Reverse: Cut 1 piece $16^1/2$in x 10in (42cm x 25.5cm) in SC 25, 2 pieces 5in x $10^1/2$ in (12.5cm x 26.5cm) in SC 04,

1 piece 4in x $10^1/2$ in (10cm x 26.5cm) in SC 08, SC 38, 1 piece 17in x $2^1/4$in (43cm x 5.75cm) in SC 08.

MAKING THE CUSHION FRONT
Start with strip 1. Take the SC 24 piece and place it right sides together so it overlaps the SC 31 piece by approx. $3/4$in (2cm) as shown in diagram a. Stitch in place and trim the SC 31 piece, (diagram b). Flip the SC 24 piece to the right side and finger press in place, (diagram c). Continue in the same way adding sections to the strip as shown in diagram d. The first three sections of SC 24 should be approx. $1/4$in - $1/2$in (0.75cm - 1.5cm) wide. Continue making the strip using the cushion assembly diagram as a guide to section widths. Don't trim the strip to length until all four strips are complete. Make up all four strips using the same method.
Note: Don't worry about wiggly seams and edges. Trim strip 1 to $2^1/2$in (6.5cm) wide, strip 2 to $1^1/2$in (4cm) wide, strip 3 to 2in (5cm) wide, strip 4 to $4^1/4$in (10.75cm).

Place the strips into position on a flat surface and adjust until none of the section seams match. Stitch together and trim the resulting panel to $7^3/4$in (19.5cm) wide by $8^3/4$in (22.25cm) high. Add the borders in the order indicated in the cushion assembly diagram.

MAKING THE CUSHION REVERSE
Stitch the 4 pieces together in the order indicated in the cushion reverse diagram. Bind the edge using the 17in x $2^1/4$in (43cm x 5.75cm) piece in SC 08. Trim the resulting rectangle to $16^1/2$in x 10in (42cm x 25.5cm).
Take the $16^1/2$in x 10in (42cm x 25.5cm) piece in SC 25, press a double $1/2$in (1.2cm) hem to the wrong side of one long edge and stitch in place, close to the first pressed edge.

FINISHING THE CUSHION
To finish the cushions follow the instruction on page 89.

Easy Peasy Cushion Assembly

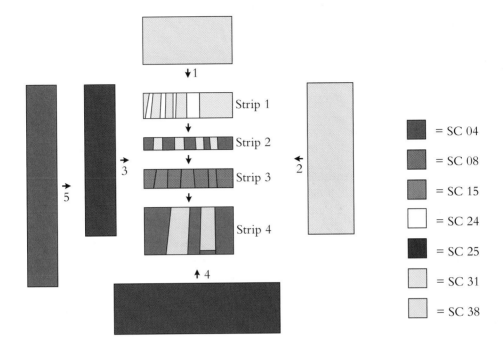

Strip 1
Strip 2
Strip 3
Strip 4

= SC 04
= SC 08
= SC 15
= SC 24
= SC 25
= SC 31
= SC 38

Easy Peasy Back

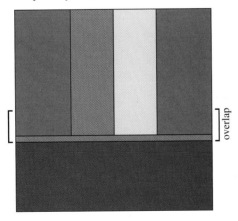

overlap

Easy Peasy Block Assembly

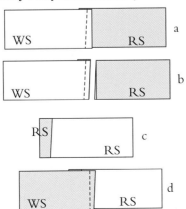

WS   RS   a

WS   RS   b

RS
RS   c

WS   RS   d

Completing the Cushions

1 Place the pieced back, face down on to the right side of the cushion front with the raw edges level.

Place the plain back, face down on top of the uncovered side of the cushion front, keeping the raw edges level and overlapping the finished edges.

2 Using a $^1/4$in (6mm) seam allowance, stitch the cushion front to the backs all around the edge.

Turn the cushion through and insert pad through the envelope style back.

Tuscan Table Runner *Pictured left*

LIZA PRIOR LUCY

W arm, sun-kissed colours of a Tuscan farmhouse punctuated by splashes of cool lilac give a Mediterranean feel to Liza's table runner.

SIZE OF QUILT
The finished runner will measure approx. 85^1/2in x 13^1/2in (217cm x 34cm).

MATERIALS
Patchwork Fabrics:
SHOT COTTON

Tangerine	SC 11:	^{1}/4yd (23cm)
Mushroom	SC 31:	^{1}/8yd (15cm)
Watermelon	SC 33:	^{1}/4yd (23cm)
Sunshine	SC 35:	^{1}/4yd (23cm)
Lilac	SC 36:	^{1}/8yd (15cm)

BROAD STRIPE

BS 11: ^{1}/2yd (45cm)

PACHRANGI STRIPE

PS 13: 1^3/4yds (1.6m) including backing and bias binding

Batting:
88in x 16in (224cm x 41cm).

Quilting thread:
Toning hand quilting thread.

Templates:
see page 94, 95

U   V

PATCH SHAPES
The table runner is comprised of two sizes of triangle (Templates U & V), which are pieced into half square triangles. The larger are in turn are pieced into pinwheel blocks for the centre section.

CUTTING OUT
Template U: Cut 5 ^{3}/8in- (13.75cm-) wide strips across the width of the fabric. Each strip will give you 14 patches per 45in- (114cm-) wide fabric. Cut 36 in BS 11, 12 in SC 11, SC 33 and SC 35.
Template V: Cut 3^1/8in- (8cm-) wide strips across the width of the fabric. Each strip will give you 26 patches per 45in- (114cm-) wide fabric. Cut 84 in PS 13, 20 in SC 11, 19 in SC 33, SC 35, 14 in SC 31 and 12 in SC 36.
Backing: Cut 2 pieces 44^1/4in x 16in (112.5cm x 41cm) in PS 13.
Bias Binding: Cut 6yds (5.5m) 2^1/2in- (6.5cm-) wide bias binding in PS 13

MAKING THE RUNNER
Using a ^{1}/4in (6mm) seam allowance throughout, referring to the runner assembly diagram for fabric combinations and stripe directions, make 9 pinwheel blocks using the larger triangles (template U) following the sequence shown in diagrams a-c. Join the smaller triangles (template V) to form 18 sets of 4 squares and add to the sides of the pinwheel blocks as shown in diagram d.
Make 2 additional sets of 6 squares for the runner ends. Assemble all the components as indicated in the runner assembly diagram.

FINISHING THE RUNNER
Press the table runner and layer with the batting and backing, baste together (see page 106). Using a toning hand quilting thread, stitch as indicated in the quilting diagram. Trim the table runner edges and attach the binding (see page107).

Table Runner Assembly

= SC 11

= SC 31

= SC 33

= SC 35

= SC 36

= BS 11

= PS 13

Block Assembly

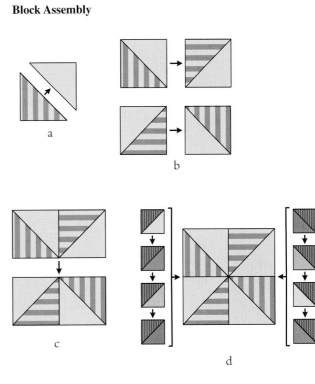

a

b

c

d

Quilting Diagram

91

Tuscan Placemats

LIZA PRIOR LUCY

M atching the Tuscan Table Runner, this set of four placemats will complete the look, of course, you can make more if you wish!

CUTTING OUT
Template V: Cut 3¹/8in- (8cm-) wide strips across the width of the fabric.
Each strip will give you 26 patches per 45in- (114cm-) wide fabric. Cut 192 in PS 13, 48 in SC 11, SC 33, SC 35, 28 in SC 36 and 20 in SC 31.
Backing: Cut 4 pieces 22in x 16in (56cm x 41cm) in PS 13.
Bias Binding: Cut 7yds (6.4m) 2¹/2in- (6.5cm-) wide bias binding in PS 13

MAKING THE PLACEMATS
Using a ¹/4in (6mm) seam allowance throughout, referring to the placemat assembly diagrams for fabric combinations and stripe directions, make 48 pinwheel blocks using triangles (template V) following the sequence shown in diagrams a-c for the Tuscan Table Runner (see page 91).
For each placemat join the pinwheel blocks into 3 rows of 4 blocks. Join the rows to form the placemats.

FINISHING THE PLACEMATS
Press the placemats.
Layer with the batting and backing, baste together (see page 106).
Using a toning hand or machine quilting thread, stitch in the ditch along the seam lines by hand or machine or copy the pattern used for the Tuscan Table Runner (see page 91).
Trim the placemat edges and attach the binding (see page 107).

To make both the Tuscan Projects you will need the following quantities of fabric:

MATERIALS
Patchwork Fabrics:
SHOT COTTON

Tangerine	SC 11:	¹/2yd (45cm)
Mushroom	SC 31:	¹/4yd (23cm)
Watermelon	SC 33:	¹/2yd (45cm)
Sunshine	SC 35:	¹/2yd (45cm)
Lilac	SC 36:	³/8yd (35cm)

BROAD STRIPE

	BS 11:	¹/2yd (45cm)

PACHRANGI STRIPE

	PS 13:	3³/4yds (3.5m) including backings and bias binding.

SIZE OF PLACEMATS
The finished placemats will measure approx. 19in x 13¹/2in (48cm x 34cm).

MATERIALS
Patchwork Fabrics:
SHOT COTTON

Tangerine	SC 11:	¹/4yd (23cm)
Mushroom	SC 31:	¹/8yd (15cm)
Watermelon	SC 33:	¹/4yd (23cm)
Sunshine	SC 35:	¹/4yd (23cm)
Lilac	SC 36:	¹/4yd (23cm)

PACHRANGI STRIPE

	PS 13:	2¹/4yds (2.1m) including backing and bias binding

Batting:
4 pieces 22in x 16in (56cm x 41cm).
Quilting Thread:
Toning hand or machine quilting thread.
Templates:
see page 94

V

PATCH SHAPES
The placemats are comprised of one triangle (Template V), which are pieced into squares, these in turn are pieced into pinwheel blocks.

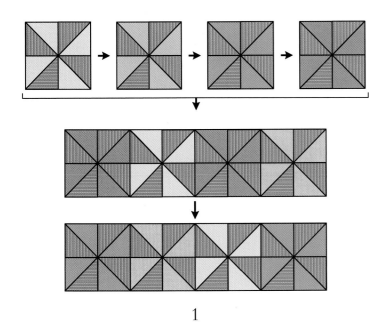

1

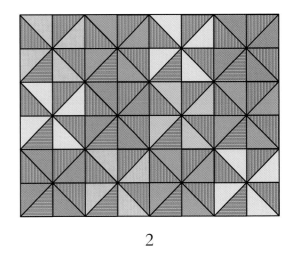

2

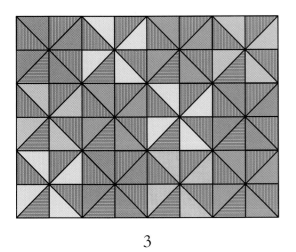

3

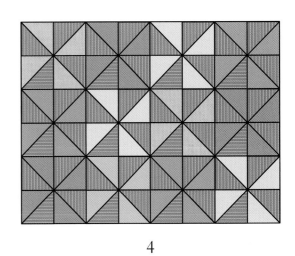

4

93

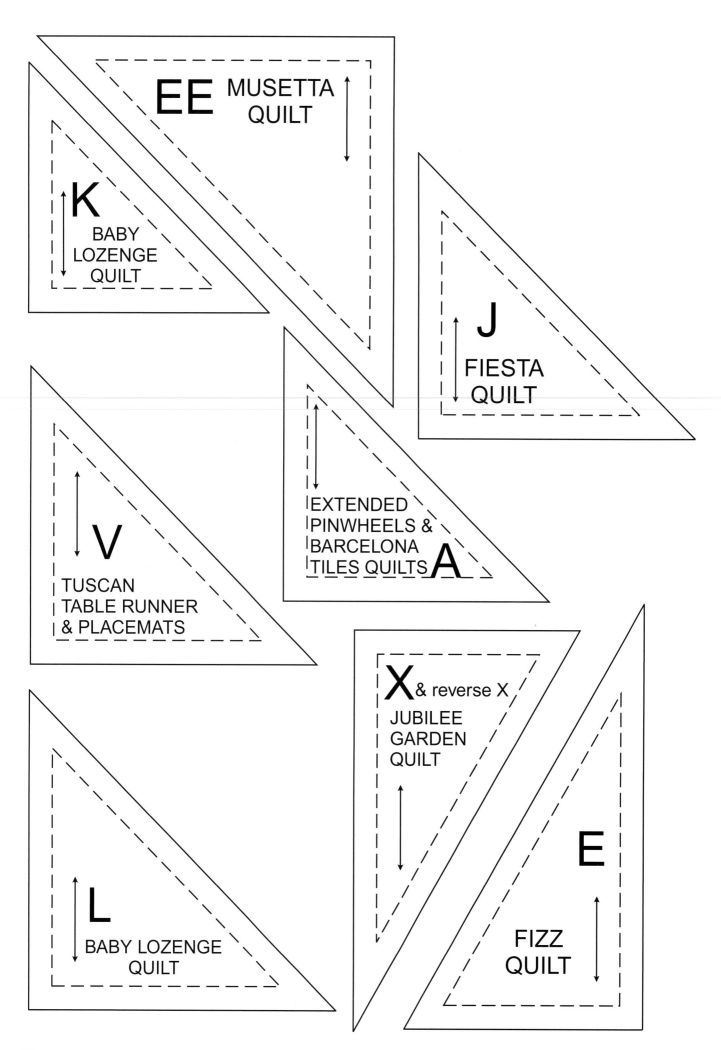

EE MUSETTA QUILT

K BABY LOZENGE QUILT

J FIESTA QUILT

V TUSCAN TABLE RUNNER & PLACEMATS

EXTENDED PINWHEELS & BARCELONA TILES QUILTS A

X & reverse X JUBILEE GARDEN QUILT

E FIZZ QUILT

L BABY LOZENGE QUILT

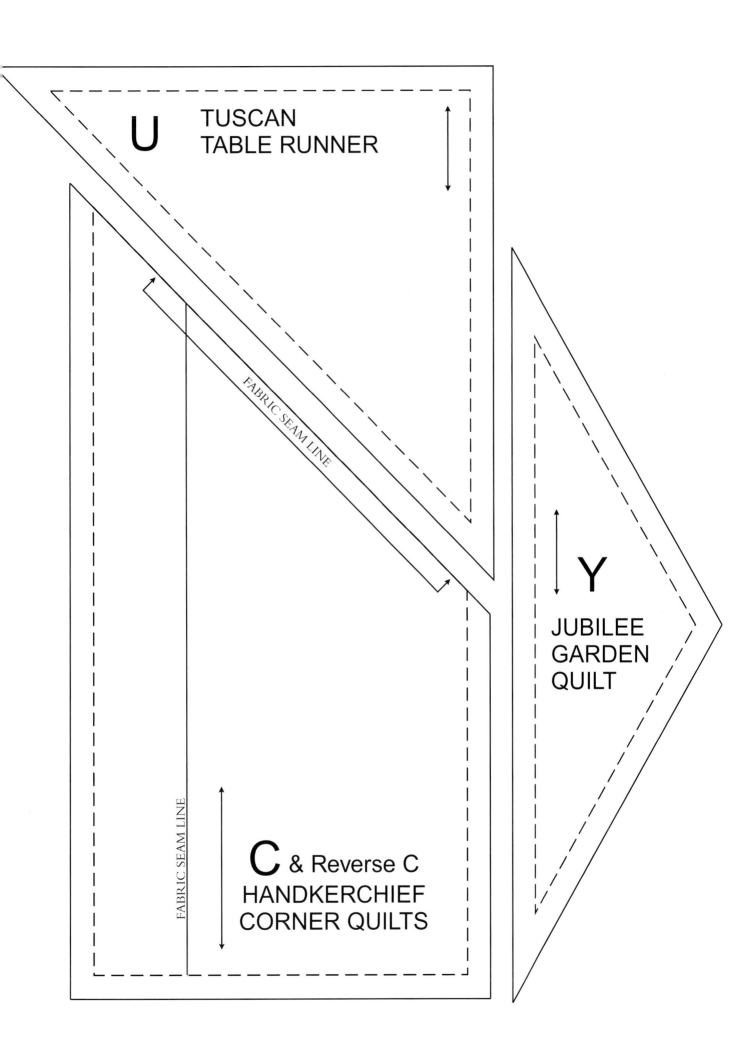

U
TUSCAN
TABLE RUNNER

FABRIC SEAM LINE

FABRIC SEAM LINE

C & Reverse C
HANDKERCHIEF
CORNER QUILTS

Y
JUBILEE
GARDEN
QUILT

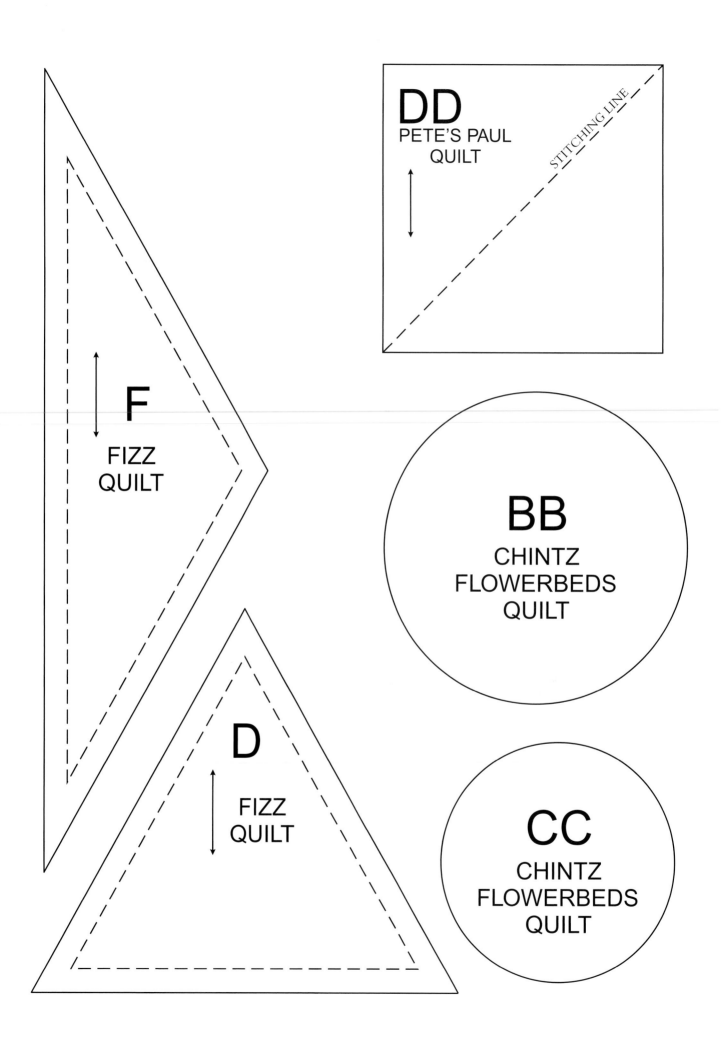

DD
PETE'S PAUL
QUILT

STITCHING LINE

F
FIZZ
QUILT

BB
CHINTZ
FLOWERBEDS
QUILT

D
FIZZ
QUILT

CC
CHINTZ
FLOWERBEDS
QUILT

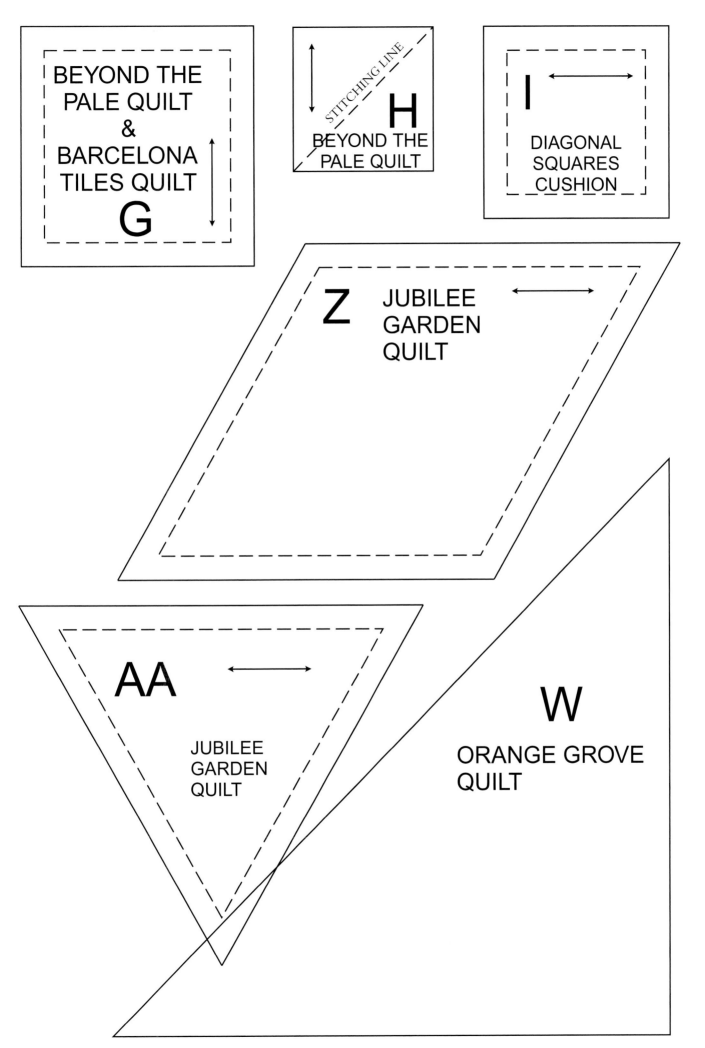

BEYOND THE
PALE QUILT
&
BARCELONA
TILES QUILT
G

STITCHING LINE
H
BEYOND THE
PALE QUILT

I
DIAGONAL
SQUARES
CUSHION

Z
JUBILEE
GARDEN
QUILT

AA
JUBILEE
GARDEN
QUILT

W
ORANGE GROVE
QUILT

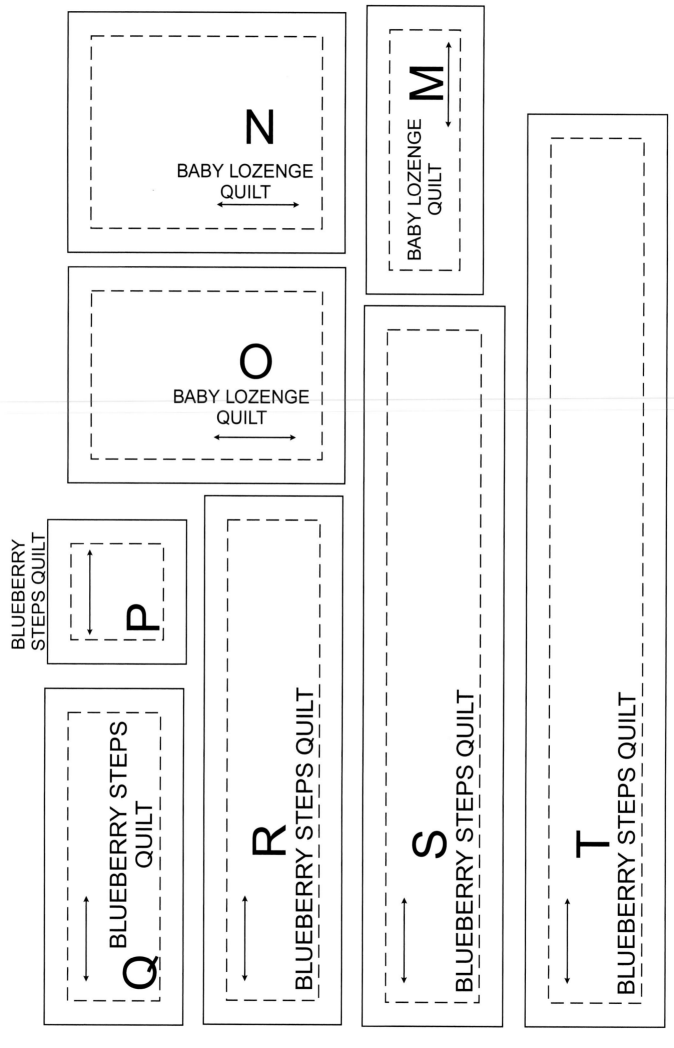

N
BABY LOZENGE
QUILT

M
BABY LOZENGE
QUILT

O
BABY LOZENGE
QUILT

P
BLUEBERRY
STEPS QUILT

Q
BLUEBERRY STEPS
QUILT

R
BLUEBERRY STEPS QUILT

S
BLUEBERRY STEPS QUILT

T
BLUEBERRY STEPS QUILT

STRIPPY CHEVRONS QUILT
EXAMPLE BLOCK 1

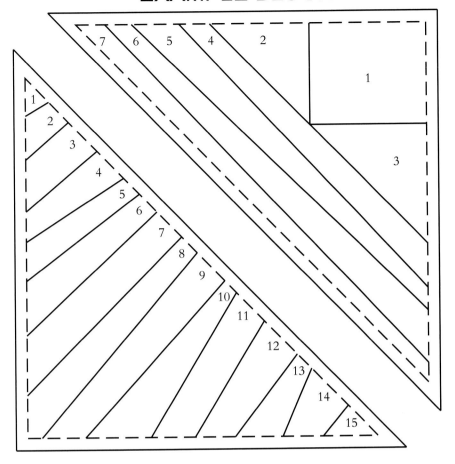

These foundation patterns are printed at 50% of real size. To use, scale them up 200% on a photocopier.

STRIPPY CHEVRONS QUILT
EXAMPLE BLOCK 2

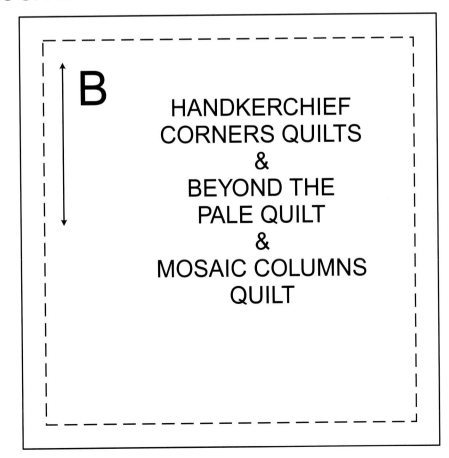

B

HANDKERCHIEF
CORNERS QUILTS
&
BEYOND THE
PALE QUILT
&
MOSAIC COLUMNS
QUILT

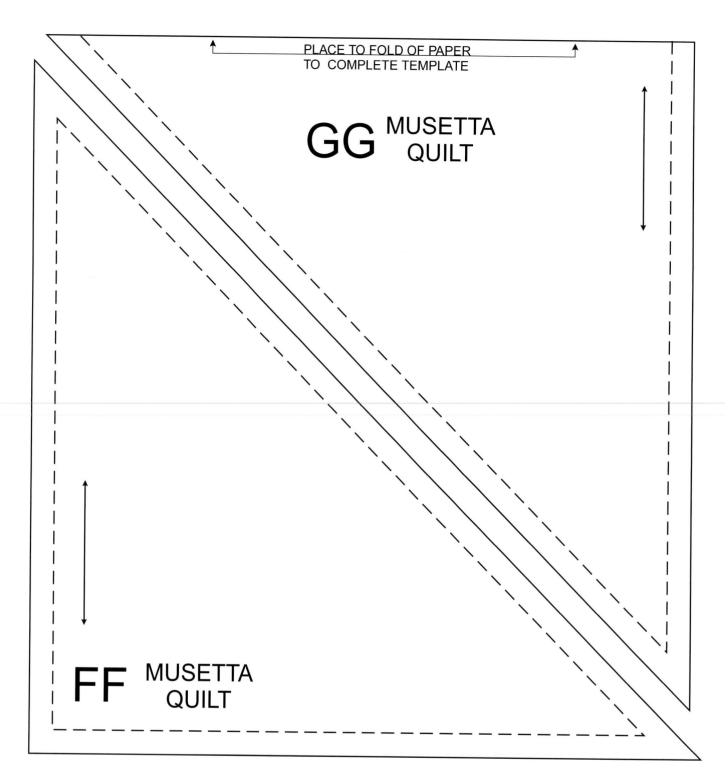

PLACE TO FOLD OF PAPER
TO COMPLETE TEMPLATE

GG MUSETTA
QUILT

FF MUSETTA
QUILT

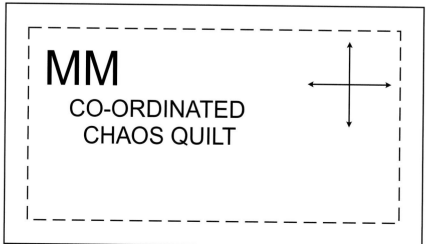

MM
CO-ORDINATED
CHAOS QUILT

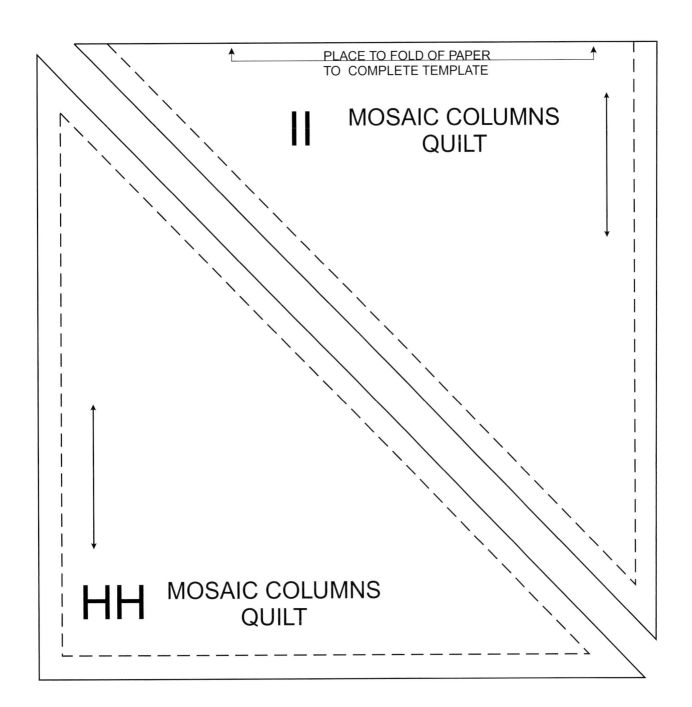

PLACE TO FOLD OF PAPER
TO COMPLETE TEMPLATE

II MOSAIC COLUMNS
QUILT

HH MOSAIC COLUMNS
QUILT

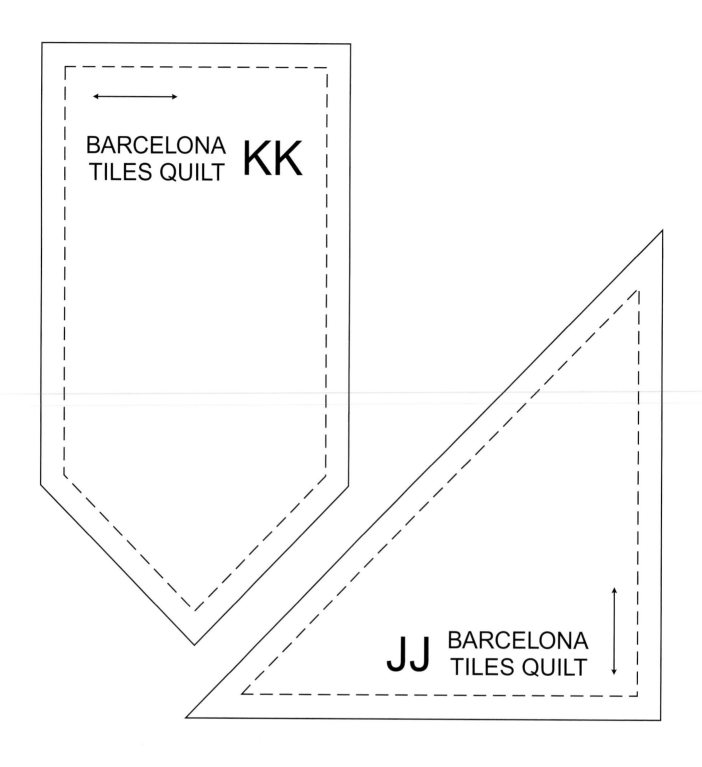

BARCELONA
TILES QUILT KK

JJ BARCELONA
TILES QUILT

BARCELONA
TILES QUILT LL

PATCHWORK KNOW-HOW

These instructions are intended for the novice quilt maker and do not cover all techniques used in making patchwork and patchwork quilts. They provide the basic information needed to make the projects in this book, along with some useful tips. Try not to become overwhelmed by technique - patchwork is a craft which should be enjoyed.

Preparing the fabric

Prewash all new fabrics before you begin, to ensure that there will be no uneven shrinkage and no bleeding of colours when the quilt is laundered. Press the fabric whilst it is still damp to return crispness to it.

Making templates

Templates are the best made from transparent template plastic, which is not only durable, but allows you to see the fabric and select certain motifs. You can also make them from thin stiff cardboard if template plastic is not available. If you choose cardboard, paint the edges of the finished template with nail polish to give it longer life.

Templates for machine-piecing

1 Trace off the actual-sized template provided either directly on to template plastic, or tracing paper, and then on to thin cardboard. Use a ruler to help you trace off the straight cutting line, dotted seam line and grainlines.

Some of the templates in this book are so large that we have only been able to give you half of them. Before transferring them on to plastic or card, trace off the half template, place the fold edge up to the fold of a piece of paper, and carefully draw around the shape. Cut out the paper double thickness, and open out for the completed template.

2 Cut out the traced off template using a craft knife, ruler and a self-healing cutting mat.

3 Punch holes in the corners of the template, at each point on the seam line, using a hole punch.

Templates for hand-piecing

• Make a template for machine piecing, but do not trace off the cutting line. Use the dotted seam line as the outer edge of the template.

• This template allows you to draw the seam lines directly on to the fabric. The seam allowances can then be cut by eye around the patch.

Cutting the fabric

On the individual instructions for each patchwork, you will find a summary of all the patch shapes used.

Always mark and cut out any border and binding strips first, followed by the largest patch shapes and finally the smallest ones, to make the most efficient use of your fabric. The border and binding strips are best cut using a rotary cutter.

Rotary cutting

Rotary cut strips are often cut across the fabric from selvedge to selvedge. With the projects we do, be certain to cut the strips running the desired direction.

1 Before beginning to cut, press out any folds or creases in the fabric. If you are cutting a large piece of fabric, you will need to fold it several times to fit the cutting mat. When there is only a single fold, place the fold facing you. If the fabric is too wide to be folded only once, fold it concertina-style until it fits your mat. A small rotary cutter with a sharp blade will cut up to 6 layers of fabric; a large cutter up to 8 layers.

2 To ensure that your cut strips are straight and even, the folds must be placed exactly parallel to the straight edges of the fabric and along a line on the cutting mat.

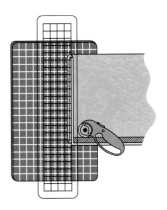

3 Place a plastic ruler over the raw edge of the fabric, overlapping it about 1/2in (1.25cm). Make sure that the ruler is at right angles to both the straight edges and the fold to ensure that you cut along the straight grain. Press down on the ruler and wheel the cutter away from yourself along the edge of the ruler.

4 Open out the fabric to check the edge. Don't worry if it's not perfectly straight; a little wiggle will not show when the quilt is stitched together. Re-fold fabric as shown in step 1, then place the ruler over the trimmed edge, aligning edge with the markings on the ruler that match the correct strip width. Cut strip along the edge of the ruler.

Using templates

The most efficient way to cut out templates is by first rotary cutting a strip of fabric the width stated for your template, and then marking off your templates along the strip, edge to edge at the required angle. This method leaves hardly any waste and gives a random effect to your patches.

A less efficient method is to fussy cut, where the templates are cut individually by placing them on particular motifs or stripes, to create special effects. Although this method is more wasteful it yields very interesting results.

1 Place the template face down on the wrong side of the fabric, with the grain line arrow following the straight grain of the fabric, if indicated. Be careful though - check with your individual instructions, as some instructions may ask you to cut patches on varying grains.

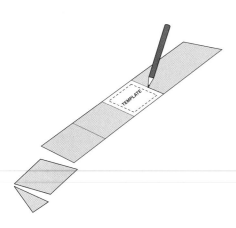

Hold the template firmly in place and draw around it with a sharp pencil or crayon, marking in the corner dots or seam lines. To save fabric, position patches close together or even touching. Don't worry if outlines positioned on the straight grain when drawn on striped fabrics do not always match the stripes when cut - this will add a degree of visual excitement to the patchwork!

3 Once you've drawn all the pieces needed, you are ready to cut the fabric, with either a rotary cutter and ruler, or a pair of sharp sewing scissors.

Basic hand- and machine-piecing

Patches can be joined together by hand or machine.
Machine stitching is quicker, but hand assembly allows you to carry your patches around with you and work on them in every spare moment. The choice is yours. For techniques that are new to you, practise on scrap pieces of fabric until you feel confident.

Machine-piecing

Follow the quilt instructions for the order in which to piece the individual patchwork blocks and then assemble the blocks together in rows.

1 Seam lines are not marked on the fabric, so stitch 1/4in (6mm) seams using the machine needle plate, a 1/4in- (6mm-) wide machine foot, or tape stuck to the machine as a guide. Pin two patches with right sides together, matching edges.

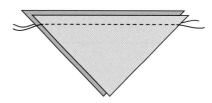

Set your machine at 10-12 stitches per inch (2.5cm) and stitch seams from edge to edge, removing pins as you feed the fabric through the machine.

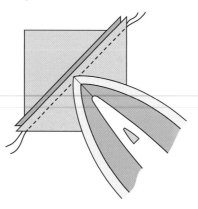

2 Press the seams of each patchwork block to one side before attempting to join it to another block.

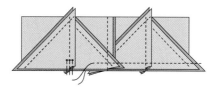

3 When joining rows of blocks, make sure that adjacent seam allowances are pressed in opposite directions to reduce bulk and make matching easier. Pin pieces together directly through the stitch line and to the right and left of the seam. Remove pins as you sew. Continue pressing seams to one side as you work.

Hand-piecing

1 Pin two patches with right sides together, so that the marked seam lines are facing outwards.

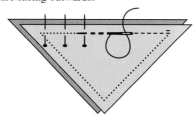

2 Using a single strand of strong thread, secure the corner of a seam line with a couple of back stitches.

3 Sew running stitches along the marked line, working 8-10 stitches per inch (2.5cm) and ending at the opposite seam line corner with a few back stitches. When hand piecing never stitch over the seam allowances.

4 Press the seams to one side, as shown in machine piecing (Step 2).

Inset seams

In some patchwork layouts a patch will have to be sewn into an angled corner formed by the joining of two other patches. Use the following method whether you are machine or hand-piecing. Don't be intimidated - this is not hard to do once you have learned a couple of techniques. The seam is sewn from the centre outwards in two halves to ensure that no tucks appear at the centre.

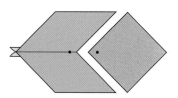

1 Mark with dots exactly where the inset will be joined and mark the seam lines on the wrong side of the fabric on the inset patch.

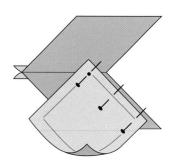

2 With right sides together and inset piece on top, pin through the dots to match the inset points. Pin the rest of the seam at right angles to the stitching line, along one edge of an adjoining patch.

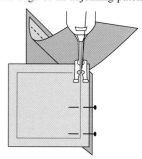

3 Stitch the patch in place along the seam line starting with the needle down through the inset point dots. Secure thread with a backstitch if hand-piecing, or stitch forward for a few stitches before backstitching, when machine-piecing.

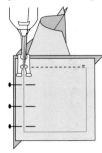

4 Pivot the patch, to enable it to align with the adjacent side of the angled corner, allowing you work on the second half of the seam. Starting with a pin at the inset point once again. Pin and stitch the second side in place, as before. Check seams and press carefully.

Free-hand Foundation Piecing - Strippy Chevrons Quilt

1 Photocopy the example blocks at 200% to make them the correct size. Trace the cutting outline and dotted stitching line of Block 1 onto 37 thin papers (1 for practice). Repeat the process to make 36 papers for Block 2.

2 Piecing Block 1: Choose a 3in (7.5cm) square and pin onto the foundation paper in the corner.

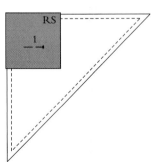

3 Take a triangle and place right sides together with the square. Check when it is folded back it will completely cover the seam allowance. Stitch.

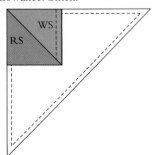

4 Fold the triangle back and press.

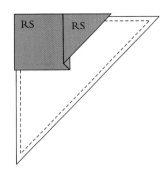

5 Repeat the process with a second triangle on the other side of the square. Trim any excess seam allowance from the centre area but leave the outside edge until the block is complete.

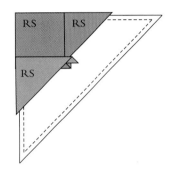

6 Place a light fabric strip right sides together with the pieced section and stitch into place.

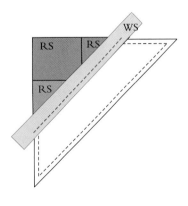

7 Fold the strip back and press.

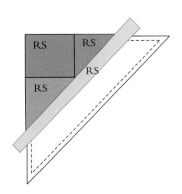

8 Follow the same procedure for the rest of the strips. When complete trim any excess fabric to the edge of the paper seam allowance. Do not remove the papers yet.

9 **Piecing Block 2:** This block is pieced using the same technique as for Block 1, using dark fabric strips.

Quilting and finishing

When you have finished piecing your patchwork and added any borders, press it carefully. It is now ready to be quilted and finished.

Preparing the backing and batting

- Remove the selvedges and piece together the backing fabric to form a backing at least 3in (7.5cm) larger all round than the patchwork top. There is no need to allow quite so much around the edges when working on a smaller project, such as a baby quilt.

- For quilting choose a fairly thin batting, preferably pure cotton, to give your quilt a flat appearance. If your batting has been rolled up, unroll it and let it rest before cutting it to the same size as the backing.

- For a large quilt it may be necessary to join 2 pieces of batting to fit. Lay the pieces of batting on a flat surface so that they overlap by approx 8in (20cm). Cut a curved line through both layers.

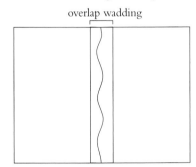

overlap wadding

- Carefully peel away the two narrow pieces and discard. Butt the curved cut edges back together. Stitch the two pieces together using a large herringbone stitch.

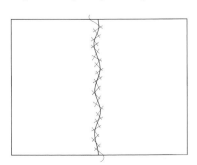

Basting the layers together

1 On a bare floor or large work surface, lay out the backing with wrong side uppermost. Use weights along the edges to keep it taut.

2 Lay the batting on the backing and smooth it out gently. Next lay the patchwork top, right side up, on top of the batting and smooth gently until there are no wrinkles. Pin at the corners and at the midpoints of each side, close to the edges.

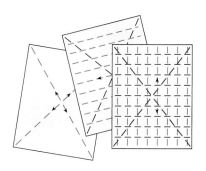

3 Beginning at the centre, baste diagonal lines outwards to the corners, making your stitches about 3in (7.5cm) long. Then, again starting at the centre, baste horizontal and vertical lines out to the edges. Continue basting until you have basted a grid of lines about 4in (10cm) apart over the entire quilt.

4 For speed, when machine quilting, some quilters prefer to baste their quilt sandwich layers together using rust-proof safety pins, spaced at 4in (10cm) intervals over the entire quilt.

Transferring quilting designs and motifs

The tool you use to mark your quilting design on to the fabric must be carefully chosen. Because of the variables of fabric in both colour, texture and fabric surface, no one marker can be recommended. It would be a terrible shame to have made your patchwork quilt up to this stage and then spoil it with bad marking! It is therefore advisable to test out various ways of marking on scrap pieces of fabric, to test how clearly you can see the marks, and whether any lines that show after stitching can be sponged or washed away.

Chalk-based markers: these include dressmakers' chalk pencils, and powdered chalk markers. These are available in a variety of colours, and leave a clear line which often disappears during stitching or is easily removed by a brush. Chalk pencils must be kept sharpened to avoid making thick lines.

Pencils: silver and soapstone pencils available from specialist shops, both produce clear lines, which are almost invisible after quilting. Coloured pencils can be used on darker fabrics, and water-erasable ones mean the lines can be sponged away after stitching.

Pale fabrics present difficulties for marking with pencils. If you choose a lead pencil, make sure it's an 'H' type, which will leave only a fine thin line.

Perforating: the design can be transferred from a paper template on to fabric by running a tracing wheel over the outlines. With many fabrics the dotted line will last long enough for work or a portion of it to be completed.

Dressmakers' carbon paper: The carbon paper is placed working side down, between the paper template and fabric. The design can then be drawn on by tracing around the design with a pencil, or running over the design with a tracing wheel to produce a dotted line. It is available in a number of colours, for both light and dark fabrics.

Quilters' tape: a narrow re-usable sticky-backed tape, which can be placed on to the fabric surface, to provide a firm guideline for quilting straight-line patterns and grids. Quilting through paper: some fabrics are difficult to mark for machine quilting. In these instances the design can be transferred on to tracing paper, which can be pinned to the surface of the quilt. The quilting is then done by stitching through the paper, which is then carefully torn away after quilting with the help of a blunt seam ripper.

Templates: some designs require templates, especially if a design is repeated. These can be used as an aid to help draw patterns either directly on to the quilt surface, or when drafting a design full-sized on to paper. With outline templates only the outside of the design can be drawn - any inner details will need to be filled in by hand.

Stencil templates can be made at home, by transferring the designs on to template plastic, or stiff cardboard. The design is then cut away in the form of long dashes, to act as guides for both internal and external lines. These templates are a quick method for producing an identical set of repeated designs.

Hand quilting

This is best done with the quilt mounted on a quilting frame or hoop, but as long as you have basted the quilt well, a frame is not necessary.

With the quilt top facing upwards, begin at the centre of the quilt and make even running stitches following the design. It is more important to make even stitches on both sides of the quilt than to make small ones.

Start and finish your stitching with back stitches and bury the ends of your threads in the batting.

Machine quilting

- For a flat looking quilt, always use a walking foot on your machine for straight lines, and a darning foot for free-motion quilting.

- It's best to start your quilting at the centre of the quilt and work out towards the borders, doing the straight quilting lines first (stitch-in-the-ditch) followed by the free-motion quilting.

- When free motion quilting stitch in a loose meandering style as shown in the diagrams. Do not stitch too closely as this will make the quilt feel stiff when finished. If you wish you can include floral themes or follow shapes on the printed fabrics for added interest.

- Make it easier for yourself by handling the quilt properly. Roll up the excess quilt neatly to fit under your sewing machine arm, and use a table, or chair to help support the weight of the quilt that hangs down the other side.

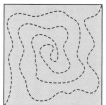

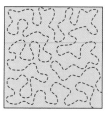

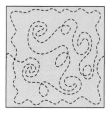

Preparing to bind the edges

Once you have quilted or tied your quilt sandwich together, remove all the basting stitches. Then, baste around the outer edge of the quilt 1/4in (6mm) from the edge of the top patchwork layer. Trim the back and batting to the edge of the patchwork and straighten the edge of the patchwork if necessary.

Making the binding

1 Cut bias or straight grain strips the width required for your binding, making sure the grainline is running the correct way on your straight grain strips. Cut enough strips until you have the required length to go

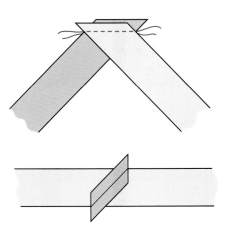

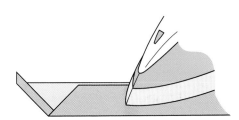

around the edge of your quilt.

2 To join strips together, the two ends that are to be joined must be cut at a 45 degree angle, as above. Stitch right sides together, trim turnings and press seam open.

Binding the edges

1 Cut starting end of binding strip at a 45-degree angle, fold a 1/4in (6mm) turning to wrong side along cut edge and press in place. With wrong sides together, fold strip in half lengthways, keeping raw edges level, and press.

2 Starting at the centre of one of the long edges, place the doubled binding on to the right side of the quilt keeping raw edges level. Stitch the binding in place starting

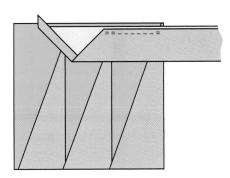

1/4in (6mm) in from the diagonal folded edge (see above). Reverse stitch to secure, and working 1/4in (6mm) in from edge of the quilt towards first corner of quilt. Stop 1/4in (6mm) in from corner and work a few reverse stitches.

3 Fold the loose end of the binding up, making a 45-degree angle (see A). Keeping the diagonal fold in place, fold the binding back down, aligning the raw edges with the next side of the quilt. Starting at the point where the last stitch ended, stitch down the next side (see B).

A

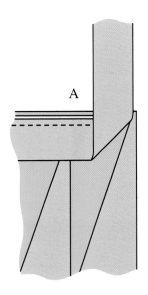

B

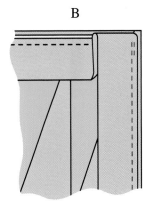

4 Continue to stitch the binding in place around all the quilt edges in this way, tucking the finishing end

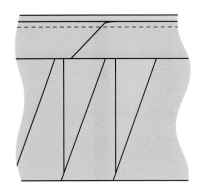

of the binding inside the diagonal starting section (see above).

5 Turn the folded edge of the binding on to the back of the quilt. Hand stitch the folded edge in place just covering binding machine stitches, and folding a mitre at each corner.

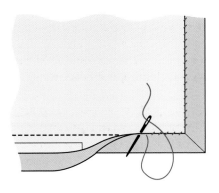

How to prepare a Quilt or Patchwork for hanging

To keep your patchwork flat when hanging on a wall, insert wooden dowels through channels at the top and base of the hanging.

To do this, cut 2 strips of fabric 1 3/4in wide (4.5cm) x the width of your quilt. Press raw edges of each strip 3/8in (1cm) to the wrong side, and then slipstitch the strips to the wrong side of the hanging at the top and base, along the long pressed edges.

Insert 3/8in- (1cm-) diameter wooden dowels cut 5cm shorter than width of quilt and slipstitch ends of channels closed. To hang the wall hanging, stitch a brass ring to each end of top channel and use to hook them over picture hooks, or nails.

GLOSSARY OF TERMS

Appliqué The technique of stitching fabric shapes on to a background to create a design. It can be applied either by hand or machine with a decorative embroidery stitch, such as buttonhole, or satin stitch.

Backing The bottom layer of a quilt sandwich. It is made of fabric pieced to the size of the quilt top with the addition of about 3in (7.5cm) all around to allow for quilting take-up.

Basting Also known as tacking in Great Britain. This is a means of holding two fabric layers or the layers of a quilt sandwich together temporarily with large hand stitches, or pins.

Batting Also known as wadding in Great Britain. Batting is the middle layer, or padding in a quilt. It can be made of cotton, wool, silk or synthetic fibres.

Bias The diagonal grain of a fabric. This is the direction which has the most give or stretch, making it ideal for bindings, especially on curved edges.

Binding A narrow strip of fabric used to finish off the edges of quilts or projects; it can be cut on the straight grain of a fabric or on the bias.

Block A single design unit that when stitched together with other blocks creates the quilt top. It is most often a square, hexagon, or rectangle, but it can be any shape. It can be pieced or plain.

Border A frame of fabric stitched to the outer edges of the quilt top. Borders can be narrow or wide, pieced or plain. As well as making the quilt larger, they unify the overall design and draw attention to the central area.

Butted corners A corner finished by stitching border strips together at right angles to each other.

Chalk pencils Available in various colours, they are used for marking lines, or spots on fabric. Some pencils have a small brush attached, although marks are easily removed.

Composite Fabric A section of fabric made by piecing other fabrics together from which patch shapes can then be cut.

Cutting mat Designed for use with a rotary cutter, it is made from a special 'self-healing' material that keeps your cutting blade sharp. Cutting mats come in various sizes and are usually marked with a grid to help you line up the edges of fabric and cut out larger pieces.

Darning foot A specialist sewing machine foot that is used in free-motion quilting - the feed dogs are disengaged so that stitches can be worked in varying lengths and directions over the fabric.

Ditch quilting Also known as quilting-in-the-ditch or stitch-in-the-ditch. The quilting stitches are worked along the actual seam lines, to give a pieced quilt texture. This is a particularly good technique for beginners as the stitches cannot be seen - only their effect.

Dressmakers' carbon paper Also known as tracing paper. Available in a number of colours, for light or dark fabric. It can be used with pencils, or a tracing wheel to transfer a quilting design on to fabric.

Feed dogs The part of a sewing machine located within the needle plate which rhythmically moves up and down to help move the fabric along while sewing.

Foundation pattern A printed base exact size of a block onto which patchwork pieces are sewn. The foundations are usually made from soft paper, but could also be lightweight fabric, interfacing, or one of the new non-woven tear-away backings, such as Stitch-n-tear.

Free-motion quilting Curved wavy quilting lines stitched in a random manner. Stitching diagrams are often given for you to follow as a loose guide.

Fussy cutting This is when a template is placed on a particular motif, or stripe, to obtain interesting effects. This method is not as efficient as strip cutting, but yields very interesting results.

Grain The direction in which the threads run in a woven fabric. In a vertical direction it is called the lengthwise grain, which has very little stretch. The horizontal direction, or crosswise grain is slightly stretchy, but diagonally the fabric has a lot of stretch. This grain is called the bias. Wherever possible the grain of a fabric should run in the same direction on a quilt block and borders.

Inset seams, setting-in or Y-seams A patchwork technique whereby one patch (or block) is stitched into a 'V' shape formed by the joining of two other patches (or blocks).

Mitred Binding A corner finished by folding and stitching binding strips at a 45-degree angle.

Mitred Borders Borders where the corners are joined at a 45-degree angle.

Needle plate The metal plate on a sewing machine, through which the needle passes via a hole to the lower part of the machine. They are often marked with lines at 1/4in (5mm) intervals, to use as stitching guides.

Padding Also known as batting in the United states and wadding in Great Britain, this is the middle layer of a quilt sandwich. Padding can be made of cotton, wool, silk or synthetic fibres and can be bought in sheets or as a loose stuffing.

Patch A small shaped piece of fabric used in the making of a patchwork pattern.

Patchwork The technique of stitching small pieces of fabric (patches) together to create a larger piece of fabric, usually forming a design.

Pieced quilt A quilt composed of patches.

Pins Use good quality pins. Do not use thick, burred or rusted pins which will leave holes or marks. Long pins with glass or plastic heads are easier to use when pinning through thick fabrics. Safety pins (size 2) can be used to 'pin-baste' the quilt layers together.

Quilters' tape A narrow removable masking tape. If placed lightly on fabric, it provides a firm guideline for straight-line patterns.

Quilting Traditionally done by hand with running stitches, but for speed modern quilts are often stitched by machine. The stitches are sewn through the top, padding and backing to hold the three layers together. Quilting stitches are usually worked in some form of design, but they can be random.

Quilting foot See walking foot.

Quilting frame A free-standing wooden frame in which the quilt layers are fixed for the entire quilting process. Provides the most even surface for quilting.

Quilting hoop Consists of two wooden circular or oval rings with a screw adjuster on the outer ring. It stabilises the quilt layers, helping to create an even tension.

Quilt sandwich Three layers of fabric: a decorative top, a middle lining or padding and a backing. Collectively known as the 'quilt sandwich'. They are held together with quilting stitches or ties.

Rotary cutter A sharp circular blade attached to a handle for quick, accurate cutting. It is a device that can be used to cut up to six layers of fabric at one time. It needs to be used in conjunction with a 'self-healing' cutting mat and a thick plastic ruler.

Rotary ruler A thick, clear plastic ruler printed with lines that are exactly 1/4in (6mm) apart. Sometimes they also have diagonal lines printed on, indicating 45 and 60-degree angles. A rotary ruler is used as a guide when cutting out fabric pieces using a rotary cutter.

Sashing A piece or pieced sections of fabric interspaced between blocks.

Sashing Posts When blocks have sashing between them the corner squares are known as sashing posts.

Selvedges Also known as selvages, these are the firmly woven edges down each side of a fabric length. Selvedges should be trimmed off before cutting out your fabric, as they are more liable to shrink when the fabric is washed. They are also difficult to quilt due to the firm nature of the weave.

Setting-in See Inset seams.

Stitch-in-the-ditch See ditch quilting.

Staystitches Rows of directional machine stitches, placed just inside certain seamlines, to prevent them from stretching out of shape during handling and construction. The most important seamlines to staystitch are those that are curved or angled. Staystitching is done immediately before or after removing your pattern, and is worked through a single layer of fabric.

Suffolk Puffs A circle of fabric double the size of the finished puff is gathered up into a rosette shape.

Tea-dyeing The use of tea for dyeing fabrics gives a subtle aged look to new fabric. Many methods can be used but there are two simple methods. For darkening and ageing specific areas of a quilt dab the area with a wet tea bag until the tea has darkened the area to your preferred level. Let the area dry, this will set the tea stain. Use very mild soap when the quilt is washed or the dyeing will fade.

For a large quilt when you want an all over effect, steep 20 tea-bags in a litre of boiling water for 20 minutes. Remove the tea-bags and pour the liquid into a dye-bath. Add warm water and mix, then add the quilt.

Let the quilt sit in the tea until it has taken the level of dye you prefer. Then remove and wash the quilt in very mild soap. It should be noted that the fabrics may be affected by the tannic acid in tea and may deteriorate earlier than normal.

Template A pattern piece used as a guide for marking and cutting out fabric patches, or marking a quilting, or appliqué design. Usually made from plastic or strong card that can be reused many times.

Threads One hundred percent cotton or cotton-covered polyester is best for hand and machine piecing. Choose a colour that matches your fabric. When sewing different colours and patterns together, choose a medium to light neutral colour, such as grey or ecru. For both hand and machine quilting it helps to use coated or pre-waxed quilting thread, which allows the thread to glide through the quilt layers. Hand quilting can be worked in special threads, such as pearl or crochet cotton.

Tracing wheel A tool consisting of a spiked wheel attached to a handle. Used to transfer a design from paper on to fabric, by running the wheel over design lines.

Tying A quick and easy way to hold the quilt sandwich layers together without using machine or hand quilting. Thread or yarn is inserted through the quilt layers at regular intervals and tied in a knot or bow, or secured with a stitch or buttons.

Unit A small part of a patchwork design made from patches, which is then pieced together with other units to form a block.

Wadding The British term for batting, or padding (inner filling).

Walking foot Also known as a quilting foot, this is a sewing machine foot with dual feed control. It is very helpful when quilting, as the fabric layers are fed evenly from the top and below, reducing the risk of slippage and puckering.

Y-seams See inset seams.

Yo-Yos See Suffolk Puffs.

Experience ratings

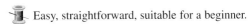 Easy, straightforward, suitable for a beginner.

 Suitable for the average pachworker and quilter

 For the more experienced patchworker and quilter.

All Drima and Sylko machine threads, Anchor embroidery threads, and Prym sewing aids, distributed in UK by Coats Crafts UK, P.O. Box 22, Lingfield House, Lingfield Point, McMullen Road, Darlington, Co. Durham, DL1 1YQ.
Consumer helpline: 01325 394237.
Anchor embroidery thread and Coats sewing threads, distributed in the USA by Coats & Clark, 4135 South Stream Blvd, Charlotte, North Carolina 28217. Tel: 704 329 5016.
Fax: 704 329 5027.
Prym products distributed in the USA by Prym-Dritz Corp, 950 Brisack Road, Spartanburg, SC 29303.
Tel: +1 864 576 5050, Fax: +1 864 587 3353, e-mail: pdmar@teleplex.net

THE KAFFE FASSETT FABRIC COLLECTION

100% Cotton
Fabric width 45ins (114cm)
Wash fabric before use

Shot Cotton

 SC 01 Ginger

 SC 02 Cassis

 SC 03 Prune

 SC 04 Slate

 SC 05 Opal

 SC 07 Persimmon

 SC 08 Raspberry

 SC 09 Pomegranate

 SC 10 Bittersweet

 SC 11 Tangerine

 SC 12 Chartreuse

 SC 14 Lavender

 SC 15 Denim Blue

 SC 16 Mustard

 SC 17 Sage

 SC 18 Tobacco

 SC 19 Lichen

 SC 20 Smoky

 SC 21 Pine

 SC 22 Pewter

 SC 23 Stone Grey

 SC 24 Ecru

 SC 25 Ginger

 SC 26 Duck Egg

 SC 27 Grass

 SC 28 Blush

 SC 31 Mushroom

 SC 32 Rosy

 SC 33 Water Melon

 SC 34 Lemon

 SC 35 Sunshine

 SC 36 Lilac

 SC 37 Coffee

 SC 38 Biscuit

 SC 39 Apple

 SC 40 Cobalt

 SC 41 Jade

SC 42 Rush

 SC 43 Lime

110

THE KAFFE FASSETT FABRIC COLLECTION

Rowan Stripe

RS 01 RS 02 RS 04 RS 05 RS 06 RS 07

Ombre Stripe

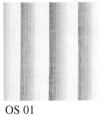   

Blue and White Stripe

 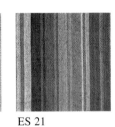

OS 01 OS 02 OS 04 OS 05 BWS 01 BWS 02

Exotic Stripe

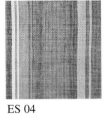  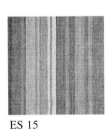  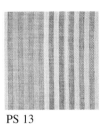 

ES 04 ES 10 ES 15 ES 16 ES 20 ES 21

Pachrangi Stripe

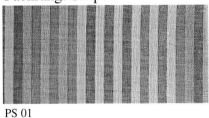   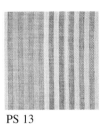 

PS 01 PS 05 PS 08 PS 13 PS 15

Narrow Stripe

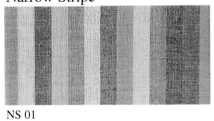 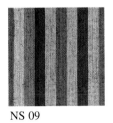   

NS 01 NS 09 NS 13 NS 16 NS 17

Broad Stripe

 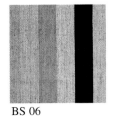   

BS 01 BS 06 BS 08 BS 11 BS 23

THE KAFFE FASSETT FABRIC COLLECTION

Alternate Stripe

AS 01

AS 03

AS 10

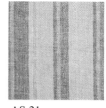

AS 21

Broad Check

BC 04

BC 02

BC 03

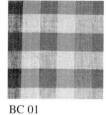

BC 01

Exotic Check

Narrow Check

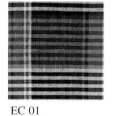

EC 01

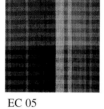

EC 05

NC 01

NC 02

NC 03

NC 05

Roman Glass

GP 01-BW

GP 01-C

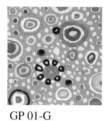

GP 01-G

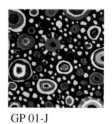

GP 01-J

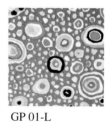

GP 01-L

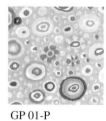

GP 01-P

Chard

GP 01-PK

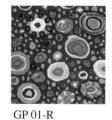

GP 01-R

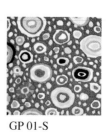

GP 01-S

GP 09-J

GP 09-L

GP O9-P

Damask

GP O2-J

GP O2-L

GP O2-P

GP O2-SM

GP O2-PG

GP O2-SA

THE KAFFE FASSETT FABRIC COLLECTION

Artichokes

GP 07-C

GP 07-J

GP 07-L

GP 07-P

Forget-me-not Rose

GP 08-C

GP 08-J

Gazania

GP03-C

GP03-L

GP03-P

GP03-S

GP03-J

Flower Lattice

GP 11-C

GP 11-J

GP 11-SU

GP 11-P

GP 11-L

Chrysanthemum

GP 13-B

GP 13-R

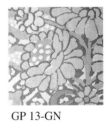
GP 13-GN

GP 13-O

GP 13-GR

FloralDance

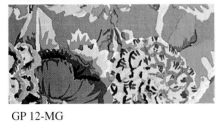
GP 12-MG

GP 12-B

GP 12-P

GP 12-O

GP 12-MV

Bubbles

GP15-P

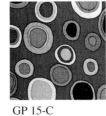
GP 15-C

GP 15-S

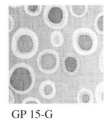
GP 15-G

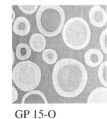
GP 15-O

113

THE KAFFE FASSETT FABRIC COLLECTION

Dotty

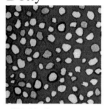 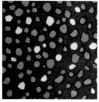 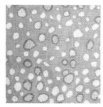 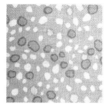 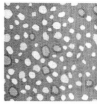 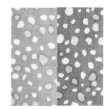

GP 14-C   GP 14-P   GP 14-O   GP 14-T   GP 14-D   GP 14-SG GP 14-L

Mosaic

GP16-PU   GP16-RG   GP16-PK   GP16-BL   GP16-GR

August Roses

GP18-PU   GP18-OC   GP18-MG   GP18-PK   GP18-PT

Peony

GP17-BL   GP17-GR   GP17-OC   GP17-TA   GP17-VI   GP17-GN

Fruit Basket

GP17-MR   GP17-RD   GP19-RD   GP19-AP   GP19-PK   GP19-BL

GP19-BK   GP19-TE   GP19-TA   GP19-GD

Please note:
The fabric swatches (shown on these pages) are not accurate in scale. To check the scale please refer to the patchwork images at the front of the book.

114

KAFFE FASSETT FABRICS USAGE LIST

Kaffe Fassett Fabric Usage List by fabric code and page number

Alternate Stripe
AS10: 60, 72
Artichokes
　GP07-C: 52, 64
　GP07-J: 60
　GP07-L: 74
　GP07-P: 52, 74, 84
August Roses
　GP18-MG: 54, 80
　GP18- PK: 54,84
　GP18-OC: 54
　GP18-PT: 69
　GP18-PU: 54, 66
Blue and White Stripe
　BWS01: 69
　BWS02: 60,69
Broad Check
　BC01: 74, 80
　BC02: 57
　BC03: 72
　BC04: 47, 72
Broad Stripe
　BS06: 82
　BS08: 47, 66
　BS11: 60, 72, 90
　BS23: 57
Bubbles
　GP15-O: 60, 74, 84
　GP15-P: 52, 60, 66, 72, 82
　GP15-G: 44, 64, 69, 74, 84
　GP15-C: 52, 72, 82
　GP15-S: 52, 82, 84
Chrysanthemum
　GP13-B: 42, 72
　GP13-O: 64, 74, 84
　GP13-R: 60, 72
　GP13-GN: 42, 64, 74
　GP13-GR: 69
Damask
　GP02-J: 54, 66, 72, 74
　GP02-L: 42
　GP02-P: 74
Dotty
　GP14-D: 44, 60, 84
　GP14-O: 44, 47, 74
　GP14-T: 69, 74
　GP14-SG: 52, 64
　GP14-P: 57, 66, 72
　GP14-L: 44, 74, 84
　GP14-C: 52, 57, 64, 66, 72
Exotic Stripe
　ES10: 72
　ES15: 52, 57
　ES16: 57

Floral Dance
　GP12-B: 52, 72
　GP12-O: 42, 72, 74, 84
　GP12-MG: 42, 54, 72, 74
　GP12-P: 42, 54, 74, 84
Flower Lattice
GP11-J: 54
Forget-Me-Not-Rose
　GP08-C: 69, 84
　GP08-J: 50, 60, 66, 74
Fruit Basket
　GP19-GD: 66
　GP19-TA: 66,80
　GP19-RD: 66, 80
　GP19-BL: 44, 69, 84
　GP19-AP: 80, 84
　GP19-PK: 44, 69
Gazania
　GP03-C: 84
　GP03-P: 66, 69, 74
　GP03-S: 69
Mosaic
　GP16-BL: 84
　GP16-PK: 47, 84
　GP16-PU: 47
　GP16-RG: 47
Narrow Check
　NC01: 72
　NC02: 57
Narrow Stripe
　NS01: 60, 72
　NS13: 66, 72
　NS16: 60
　NS17: 72
Ombre Stripe
　OS01: 69
　OS02: 69, 84
　OS04: 44
　OS05: 44, 69, 74
Pachrangi Stripe
　PS01: 47, 52, 57
　PS05: 47
　PS08: 72
　PS13: 90, 92
Peony
　GP17-GR: 44, 69, 84
　GP17-TA: 69
　GP17-Vi: 69, 84
　GP17-BL: 44, 84
　GP17-MR: 66, 72
　GP17-GN: 42, 74
　GP17-OC: 84
　GP17-RD: 84
Roman Glass
　GP01-BW: 44, 52, 64, 72

GP01-C: 60, 72, 82
GP01-G: 47, 66, 72, 74
GP01-J: 60, 82
GP01-L: 72, 74, 84
GP01-P: 69, 82
GP01-PK: 60, 84
GP01-R: 54, 60, 72, 82
Rowan Stripe
　RS01: 42, 66
　RS02: 52, 64
　RS04: 60, 66
　RS05: 52, 60, 66, 84
　RS06: 74
　RS07: 60, 64
Shot Cotton
　SC01: 60, 76
　SC02: 57, 66, 76
　SC03: 57
　SC04: 86, 88
　SC05: 42, 44, 57, 60
　SC07: 64
　SC08: 42, 60, 86, 88
　SC09: 47, 60
　SC10: 60
　SC11: 42, 60, 66, 76
　SC12: 57, 60, 66, 76
　SC14: 42, 44, 57, 60, 64, 66
　SC15: 57, 66, 86, 88
　SC16: 42, 60, 76
　SC17: 76
　SC18: 76
　SC19: 76
　SC20: 57
　SC21: 57, 76
　SC22: 57, 76
　SC23: 76
　SC24: 44, 76, 88
　SC25: 86, 88
　SC26: 42, 44, 60, 76
　SC27: 57, 76
　SC28: 44
　SC31: 42, 52, 66, 86, 88, 90, 92
　SC32: 60
　SC33: 42, 54, 86, 88, 90, 92
　SC34: 76
　SC35: 76, 82, 90, 92
　SC36: 42, 44, 64, 90, 92
　SC37: 42
　SC38: 86, 88
　SC39: 64, 76
　SC40: 42, 57, 64
　SC41: 54,57,64
　SC42: 76, 82
　SC43: 42, 76
See pages 110-114 for full fabric range

FABRIC CODES

The following information is for the Rowan global distributors and retailers, excluding the USA. The fabric codes in the left hand column are the codes used in this book; the codes in the right hand column are for use when ordering fabric.

Codes Used in This Book	Ordering Code
Shot Cotton	
SC 01	SC001
SC 02	SC002
SC 03	SC003
SC 04	SC004
SC 05	SC005
SC 07	SC007
SC 08	SC008
SC 09	SC009
SC 10	SC010
SC 11	SC011
SC 12	SC012
SC 14	SC014
SC 15	SC015
SC 16	SC016
SC 17	SC017
SC 18	SC018
SC 19	SC019
SC 20	SC020
SC 21	SC021
SC 22	SC022
SC 23	SC023
SC 24	SC024
SC 25	SC025
SC 26	SC026
SC 27	SC027
SC 28	SC028
SC 31	SC031
SC 32	SC032
SC 33	SC033
SC 34	SC034
SC 35	SC035
SC 36	SC036
SC 37	SC037
SC 38	SC038
SC 39	SC039
SC 40	SC040
SC 41	SC041
SC 42	SC042
SC 43	SC043
Rowan Stripe	
RS 01	RS001
RS 02	RS002
RS 04	RS004
RS 05	RS005
RS 06	RS006
RS 07	RS007
Ombre Stripe	
OS 01	OS001
OS 02	OS002

Codes Used in This Book	Ordering Code
OS 04	OS004
OS 05	OS005
Blue & White Stripe	
BWS 01	BWS01
BWS 02	BWS02
Alternate Stripe	
AS 01	AS001
AS 03	AS003
AS 10	AS010
AS 21	AS021
Pachrangi Stripe	
PS 01	PS001
PS 05	PS005
PS 08	PS008
PS 13	PS013
PS 15	PS015
Broad Stripe	
BS 01	BS001
BS 06	BS006
BS 08	BS008
BS 11	BS011
BS 23	BS023
Narrow stripe	
NS01	NS001
NS09	NS009
NS13	NS013
NS16	NS016
NS17	NS017
Exotic Stripe	
ES04	ES004
ES10	ES010
ES15	ES015
ES16	ES016
ES20	ES020
ES21	ES021
Exotic Check	
EC 01	EC001
EC 05	EC005
Narrow Check	
NC 01	NC001
NC 02	NC002
NC 03	NC003
NC 05	NC005
Broad check	
BC 01	BC001
BC 02	BC002

Codes Used in This Book	Ordering Code
BC 03	BC003
BC 04	BC004
Roman Glass	
GP01-BW	G01BW
GP01-C	G01CR
GP01-G	G01GD
GP01-J	G01JW
GP01-L	G01LF
GP01-P	G01PT
GP01-PK	G01PK
GP01-R	G01RD
GP01-S	G01ST
Damask	
GP02-J	G02JW
GP02-L	G02LF
GP02-P	G02PT
Gazania	
GP03-C	G03CR
GP03-J	G03JW
GP03-L	G03LF
GP03-P	G03PT
GP03-S	G03ST
Artichokes	
GP07-C	G07CR
GP07-J	G07JW
GP07-L	G07LF
GP07-P	G07PT
Forget me Not Rose	
GP08-C	G08CR
GP08-J	G08JW
Chard	
GP09-J	G09JW
GP09-L	G09LF
GP09-P	G09PT
Flower Lattice	
GP11-C	G11 CR
GP11-J	G11 JW
GP11-L	G11 LF
GP11-SU	G11 SU
GP11-P	G11 PT
Floral Dance	
GP12-B	G12BL
GP12-O	G12OC
GP12-MG	G12MG
GP12-MV	G12MV
GP12-P	G12PK
Chrysanthemum	
GP13-B	G13BL

Codes Used in This Book	Ordering Code
GP13-O	G13OC
GP13-R	G13RD
GP13-GN	G13GN
GP13-GR	G13GR
Dotty	
GP14-D	G14DR
GP14-O	G14OC
GP14-T	G14TR
GP14-SG	G14SG
GP14-P	G14PL
GP14-L	G14LV
GP14-C	G14CB
Bubbles	
GP15-O	G15OC
GP15-P	G15PL
GP15-G	G15GR
GP15-C	G15CB
GP15-S	G15SB
Mosaic	
GP16-BL	G16BL
GP16-PK	G16PK
GP16-GR	G16GR
GP16-RG	G16RD
GP16-PU	G16PU
Peony	
GP17-OC	G17OC
GP17-TA	G17TA
GP17-GR	G17GR
GP17-VI	G17VI
GP17-RD	G17RD
GP17-MR	G17MR
GP17-GN	G17GN
GP17-BL	G17BL
August Roses	
GP18-PT	G18PT
GP18-PK	G18PK
GP18-OC	G18OC
GP18-MG	G18MG
GP18-PU	G18PU
Fruit Basket	
GP19-RD	G19RD
GP19-GD	G19GD
GP19-BK	G19BK
GP19-AP	G19AP
GP19-TA	G19TA
GP19-TE	G19TE
GP19-PK	G19PK
GP19-BL	G19BL

DISTRIBUTORS AND STOCKISTS

Overseas Distributors of Rowan Fabrics

AUSTRALIA
Sunspun
185 Canterbury Road
Canterbury 3126

VICTORIA
Tel : 61 3 9830 1609
E mail : admin@sunspun.com.au

CANADA
Westminster Fibers Inc
4 Townsend West
Suite 8,
Nashua
New Hampshire 03063
Tel : 603 886 5041
E - mail : wfibers@aol.com

BELGIUM
Rhinetex
Geurdeland 7
6673 DR Andelst
Tel : 31 488 480030

DENMARK
Industrial Textiles
Engholm Parkvej 1
DK 3450 ALLERØD
Tel : 45 48 17 20 55
E mail : mail@indutex.dk

FINLAND
Coats Opti OY
Ketjutie 3
04220 KERAVA
Tel : 358 9 274 871

FRANCE
Rhinetex
Geurdeland 7
6673 DR Andelst
Tel : 31 488 480030

GERMANY
Rhinetex
Geurdeland 7
6673 DR Andelst
Tel : 31 488 480030

ICELAND
Malin Orglygsdottir
Garnverslunin Storkurinn
Kjorgardi Laugavegi 59
101 Reykjavik
Tel : 354 551 82 58.

ITALY
D.L SRL
Via Piave 24 - 26
20016 PERO
MILANO
Tel : 39 02 339 10 180

JAPAN
Lecien Corporation
Art & Hobby Division
3F 15 Takeda Tobadono-Cho
Fushimi- Ku
Kyoto
Tel : 81 75 623 3805

NEW ZEALAND
Alterknitives,
PO Box 47961,
Auckland
Tel : (64) 9 376 0337

NORWAY
Industrial Textiles
Engholm Parkvej 1
DK 3450 ALLERØD
Tel : 45 48 17 20 55
E mail : mail@indutex.dk

SOUTH KOREA
Elgatex
143-1, Sinsa- Dong
Enpyung-ku
Seoul
Tel : 82 17 265 0730

SPAIN
Lucretia Beleta Patchwork
Dr Rizal 12
08006 Barcelona
Tel : 34 93 41 59555

SWITZERLAND
Rhinetex
Geurdeland 7
6673 DR Andelst
Tel : 31 488 480030

SWEDEN
Industrial Textiles
Engholm Parkvej 1
DK 3450 ALLERØD
Tel : 45 48 17 20 55
E mail : mail@indutex.dk

TAIWAN
Long T eh Trading Co
Rm 920, 9F - 10
No 68, Sec 4, Jen A1 Road
Taipei
Tel : 886 2 2705 4491

UK
Rowan
Green Lane Mill
Holmfirth
West Yorkshire
England, HD9 2DX
Tel : +44(0) 1484 681881
Internet : www.knitrowan.com
Email : Mail@knitrowan.com

U.S.A
Westminster Fibers Inc
4 Townsend West
Suite 8,
Nashua
New Hampshire 03063
Tel : 603 886 5041
E - mail : wfibers@aol.com

OTHER ROWAN TITLES AVAILABLE

Patchwork and Quilting
Book Number One
£7.50

Patchwork and Quilting
Book Number Two
£9.95

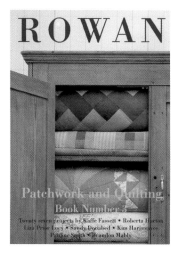

Patchwork and Quilting
Book Number Three
£10.95

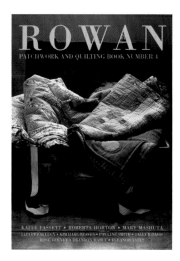

Patchwork and Quilting
Book Number Four
£12.95

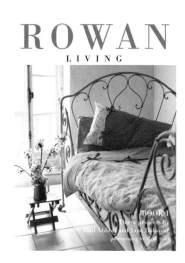

Rowan Living
Book One
£12.95

Rowan Creative Living
Book Two
£12.95

ROWAN

Green Lane Mill, Holmfirth, West Yorkshire, England
Tel: +44 (0) 1484 681881   Fax: +44 (0) 1484 687920   Internet: www.knitrowan.com
Email: Mail@knitrowan.com

INDEX